MESSAGE OF BIBLICAL SPIRITUALITY

Editorial Director: Carolyn Osiek, RSCJ

Volume 5

The Wisdom Literature

Kathleen M. O'Connor

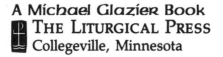

A Michael Glazier Book
THE LITURGICAL PRESS
Collegeville, Minnesota

Illustrations by Gretchen M. Griesmer
Cover design by Florence Bern

A Michael Glazier Book published by The Liturgical Press

1   2   3   4   5   6   7   8

Library of Congress Cataloging-in-Publication Data

O'Connor, Kathleen M., 1942–
    The Wisdom literature / Kathleen M. O'Connor.
        p.   cm. — (Message of biblical spirituality ; v. 5)
    Includes bibliographical references and index.
    ISBN 0-8146-5571-8
    1. Wisdom literature—Criticism, interpretation, etc.   I. Title.
II. Series.
BS1455.034   1993
223'.06—dc20   92-43852
                                                                  CIP

To my father,
W. Vincent O'Connor,
for his inspiration and love,
and in loving memory of my mother,
Kathleen Dunn O'Connor,
who even in death,
"laughed at the days to come."

TABLE OF CONTENTS

EDITOR'S PREFACE

One of the characteristics of church life today is a revived interest in spirituality. There is a growing list of resources in this area, yet the need for more is not exhausted. People are yearning for guidance in living an integrated life of faith in which belief, attitude, affections, prayer, and action form a cohesive unity which gives meaning to their lives.

The biblical tradition is a rich resource for the variety of ways in which people have heard God's call to live a life of faith and fidelity. In each of the biblical books we have a witness to the initiative of God in human history and to the attempts of people not so different from ourselves to respond to the revelation of God's love and care.

The fifteen volumes in the *Message of Biblical Spirituality* series aim to provide ready access to the treasury of biblical faith. Modern social science has made us aware of how the particular way in which one views reality conditions the ways in which one will interpret experience and life itself. Each volume in this series is an attempt to retell and interpret the biblical story from within the faith perspective that originally formed it. Each seeks to portray what it is like to see God, the world, and oneself from a particular point of view and to search for ways to respond faithfully to that vision. We who are citizens of our twentieth century world cannot be people of the ancient biblical world, but we can grow closer to their experience and their faith and thus closer to God, through the living Word of God which is the Bible.

The series includes an international group of authors representing England, Ireland, Canada, and the United States, but whose life experience has included first-hand knowledge of many other countries. All are proven scholars and committed believers whose faith is as important to them as their scholarship. Each acts as interpreter of one part of the biblical tradition in order to enable its spiritual vitality to be passed on to others. It is our hope that through their labor the reader will be able to enter more deeply into the life of faith, hope, and love through a fuller understanding of and appreciation for the biblical Word as handed down to us by God's faithful witnesses, the biblical authors themselves.

Carolyn Osiek, RSCJ
Associate Professor of New Testament Studies
Catholic Theological Union, Chicago

ACKNOWLEDGEMENTS

The wisdom literature took hold of me years ago and it has never relinquished its grasp. To all those who have taught me wisdom, who have joined me in the search for Wisdom, and who have assisted me in the struggle to write about wisdom, I give thanks:

To the sagacious and gifted teacher who first introduced me to the wisdom literature, Helen O'Neill, O.P., Professor of Biblical Studies, Providence College, Providence, Rhode Island, from whom I caught a breath of spirit.

To my students at the Maryknoll School of Theology, and in particular, those in my wisdom classes, whose curiosity, insights, and struggles have instructed me about the wisdom books and about the global realities to which the vision of wisdom speaks.

To the librarians at the Maryknoll School of Theology, to Jim O'Halloran and Peggy Mayti, for tracking down materials from libraries near and far, and to Jim and Zay Green, for conducting a bibliographical hunt worthy of a mystery novel.

To my colleague and friend, Miriam Frances Perlewitz, M.M., for loving companionship in the pain and the delight of this enterprise.

To all my family, old and new, for their love and encouragement, especially to Gretchen Griesmer, for her artistic contributions, and to my sister, Margy O'Keefe, for a critical reading of some of the chapters.

To my husband, Jim Griesmer, for the thousand and one practical things he did to help me write this book, but above all for his love, his laughter, and his patient wisdom, as I searched for order in the chaos.

INTRODUCTION

A Spirituality for the Market Place

The market places were the centers of public life in the towns and villages of the Ancient Near East. Nearly everything that was important to the community happened there. Besides serving as places of exchange for the ordinary foods and products necessary for daily survival, the market places also functioned as gathering spots for the community. There friends met, news was exchanged and legal and political decisions were made. Bustling, crowded spaces filled with noises and smells, the market places contained life at its most promising and its most mundane. In them deals were made, fortunes won and lost and people struggled to survive.

This volume treats the following six books as the wisdom literature of the Old Testament: Proverbs, Job, Qoheleth and the Song of Songs, Sirach and the Wisdom of Solomon. Though in these books the image of the market place or public square occurs infrequently (Provs 1:20; 7:12: and perhaps in 8:2), its theological value extends far beyond the paucity of its appearances. As a poetic and theological image the market place expresses the fascination of the wisdom thinkers with ordinary human existence. It represents the arena where humans struggle to cope with the chaos of daily life, where Wisdom and Folly compete for human loyalties, and where the divine and the human meet.

For most of us, a spirituality, if it is to make any sense at all, must be an indigenous child of the market place, a native of the world of economic and social exchange. Most people live in a swirling chaos of claims upon them, to feed the family, to pay the bills, and to meet faithfully the requirements of work and of love. Indeed, most of the world's peoples contend mightily for their daily bread and barely eke out a subsistence. A spirituality that is native to the market place understands human life itself as the hallowed place. It comes to know that the most mundane of human efforts and the loftiest of human aspirations are integral to the life of the spirit as marrow is to the bones.

A spirituality for the market place has two tasks: to uncover the sacred in life's confusion and ambiguity, and to make possible prayer and praise in the tumbling profusion of daily existence. For inhabitants of the market place, anything less will make no sense, give little energy, and leave us fragmented and bereft.

What is Spirituality?

A biblical scholar named Sean McEvenue identifies two components of authentic spirituality.[1] He suggests, first, that true spiritualities point to a realm or sphere of life wherein humans might expect to meet God, such as in church, at work, or among the poor. McEvenue observes further that spirit-

---

[1] "The Spirituality of the Bible," a paper presented at the annual meeting of the Catholic Biblical Associaton, Loyola University, New Orleans, 1984.

ualities teach a stance toward life or a way to live in the world, for example, through disciplined prayer, through mortification of the body or through social action. Though the various spiritualities may have much in common, they can usually be distinguished from one another on the basis of these two descriptive categories. The biblical wisdom literature makes specific claims about divine-human relationship that allow its perspective to be named a spirituality. Wisdom understands the realm of divine-human encounter to be ordinary human life, and it teaches that the way to stand in the world, the stance to adopt before reality, is the way of relationship.

The Realm

At first glance there seems to be nothing too surprising about wisdom's claim that the arena where God comes to meet us is daily life. Common sense confirms it. However, a great deal of spiritual thinking affirms another, separate sphere of existence, an elite world of sacred places and guaranteed silences. Of course, spiritualities that restrict God's activity so narrowly distort the great classical spiritual traditions, including those conceived in monasteries and religious communities.

Nonetheless, much popular thinking limits divine-human exchange to specifically religious activities and places, and it claims that God is found primarily in the privacy of the individual soul.[2] A spirituality that encourages withdrawal from community and flight from the world is simply not adequate to life today. The wisdom literature provides a resource for a more holistic spirituality, one that perceives outer and inner life, individual and community life and God and the world as inextricably intertwined.

A Creation Theology

Wisdom spirituality accepts, indeed, blesses, life in the market place. It takes everyday existence with the utmost seriousness. It asserts that ordinary human life, here and now, in all its beauty, ambiguity and pain, are of immense importance to human beings and to their Creator. In wisdom's view the struggles and conflicts of daily life are not to be escaped but embraced in full consciousness of their revelatory and healing potential.

The reason for this view is wisdom's underlying assumption that all of creation exists in the presence of its Creator. The whole realm of existence, from the ants to the constellations, from plant life to human life, forms an organic unity that is the sacred work of God. Anything that occurs in the dwelling place of humans comes under the care, concern and saving possibilities of its Designer. Consequently, ordinary life and the life of faith are not two separate spheres but one unified experience of God's creation.[3] When Israel's wisdom literature

[2]See Gustavo Gutierrez's analysis of this popular thinking in *We Drink from Our Own Wells* (Maryknoll: Orbis, 1984) 13-16.

[3]See Hans-Jurgen Hermission, "Observations on the Creation Theology in Wisdom" in *Creation in the Old Testament*, ed. Bernhard W. Anderson, Issues in Religion and Theology 6 (Philadelphia: Fortress, 1984) 118-134.

concentrates intensely on mundane human concerns, it is not ignoring faith but assuming it.

Wisdom's concentration on human concerns, on the one hand, and its seeming inattention to specifically religious and theological matters, on the other, has caused many biblical interpreters to question the presence of this literature in the Bible at all. As a result, the wisdom books have stood in the shadows of the Old Testament, "irreligious" orphans next to their more theological siblings, the prophets, the pentateuch and the historical books.

Against these accusations one prominent wisdom scholar, Roland E. Murphy,[4] defends wisdom's viewpoint by referring to it as "theological anthropology." Because wisdom's starting point is the realm of human experience, from the most trivial daily concerns to the most sublime questions of human suffering and meaning, that does not mean that it excludes God from its world. Instead, wisdom focuses on what it means to be human before God. Murphy maintains further that the modern distinction between the realms of the secular and the sacred never existed in Israel. Wisdom does not impose God on life but assumes God's presence and activity in every facet of its existence.

A Way to Stand

If the wisdom literature is slow to discuss God and matters

---

[4]Roland E. Murphy's most recent thinking on this subject is presented in "Wisdom-Theses and Hypotheses" in *Israelite Wisdom: Theological and Literary Essays in Honor of Samuel Terrien,* ed. John G. Gammie, et al. (New York: Union Theological Seminary, 1978) 35-42; and in "Wisdom and Creation," *Journal of Biblical Literature,* 104/1 (March 1985) 3-11.

usually termed religious, it is not at all timid in advising its adherents about how to conduct their lives. Broadly speaking, the six books addressed in this volume all urge their readers, directly or indirectly, to live in harmonious relationships with the community, with the earth and with the Creator. If one would be wise, no aspect of reality is excluded from this matrix of relationships. To become wise requires recognition of and full participation in this interlocking set of connections with others, with the created world and with God.

The Purpose of This Volume

My first purpose in this volume is to attempt to expose the spiritualities, implicit or explicit, of the wisdom books of the Old Testament. To do so requires crossing the centuries to enter into the experience and thought of the ancient communities that produced the literature and, therefore, to understand, as far as possible, its original significance for them. However, in doing so my criteria for selecting which themes to highlight and which to ignore arise from my own assumptions and convictions about life today. My second purpose and the goal of this work is to explore the vast and frequently overlooked resource that the wisdom literature provides for contemporary believers.[5]

These two purposes are related but distinct. The first involves an historical and literary task, the second, an imaginative and dialogical one. The effort to understand the books as

[5] I am grateful to William H. Irwin, CSB, whose paper "Biblical Spirituality as and Object of Biblical Research" (presented at the annual meeting of the Old Testament Colloquium, Conception Seminary College, December, 1986), helped me clarify my thinking on these matters.

historically anchored recognizes that God's word to the believing community is shaped in and by the concreteness of specific historical contexts. To ignore these contexts is to imperil the scandalous truth that God speaks in human history. However, to leave the word dormant in its historical setting without regard to the circumstances of the interpreter and her community is to place the bibical text in a glass box in a museum.

In addition to the wisdom literature's focus on human experience as the starting point for theology and its emphasis on relationship as the way of holiness, four related themes recur throughout the literature that may have particular importance for the believing communities in North America today.

Ambiguity as Revelatory

Because the wisdom literature appreciates the ambiguity of human experience, it struggles against rote religious answers to human problems. Furthermore, it sees in ambiguity and confusion the opportunity for breakthrough into mystery. To an age enamored of technological thinking, it recalls and reaffirms the existence of transcendent mystery.

According to wisdom, life is not a simple set of truths to be followed scrupulously, but a continual encounter with conflicting truths, each making competing claims upon the seeker. Wisdom views life as paradoxical, requiring discernment from situation to situation of how, when and if one should act. The sages express this perception of reality in both the content and the form of the literature. The subject matter of Proverbs, Job and Ecclesiastes, and even the Song of Songs, is each in its own way profoundly ambiguous and paradoxical. Opposing truths are set side by side, and in some instances not resolved at all. This requires that readers enter into the ambiguity themselves and discover their own resolutions to the conflict of truths.

Furthermore, the sages express the flavor of their subject matter even in their choice of literary forms. The basic literary genre of wisdom is the *mashal*. A *mashal* is a comparison, short saying, proverb or sometimes a riddle, which expresses a truth about life in concrete, succinct images. For the sages, particularly the writers of Proverbs, a collection of *mashalim* (the plural form of the noun and the Hebrew title of the Book), life itself is a *mashal*, a world of ambiguity, a series of puzzles small and great. These must be met with openness, with discernment and with the aide of the experience of those wiser than oneself. The point of highlighting ambiguity or paradox is not to bring the individual to an intellectual impasse but to lead her beyond the obvious into deeper, transcendent truth. Consequently, wisdom offers a spirituality of discovery, requiring vigilance and choice.

Suffering and Justice

Reflection on the irruption of evil into human life led the sages to question why, repeatedly in human life, evil annihilates the good. In the Books of Job and Ecclesiastes, and then later in the Book of the Wisdom of Solomon, the ambiguity which characterizes human life takes on particularly sinister colors. The questions of why the innocent suffer, why anyone suffers at all, are set squarely against the consistent but contradictory belief of Israel that God is a just God. Ultimately in this literature it is God who is placed on trial. Can God be just and inflict evil or even allow evil to befall humanity? This question is the macro-riddle of the wisdom literature and, perhaps, of life throughout the bloody smear that is our century.

The Wisdom Woman

Another theme revolves around the figure of personified wisdom. In an age when exclusively male images of the divine are being radically questioned as idolatrous representations of maleness, the wisdom literature offers a pool of images and visions in which divine reality and relationship are expressed in female images. In the contemporary struggle to glimpse God through new language, the wisdom literature offers an untapped spring of words and symbols for the divine. This language may help us glimpse the transcendent mystery of God in new ways and, thus, to grasp with equal newness our own identities as human beings.

A Theology of Community

In focusing on human experience, the wisdom literature places great priority on the life of the community over the individual. In many ways this vision could serve as an antidote to the harsh and competitive individualism that characterizes life in most of North American culture. Though wisdom attends carefully to the interests of the individual, it is always in the context of the enhancement of the life of the whole community. Anything that will promote that life, its harmony, its joy and its satisfaction, is agreeable to wisdom. To express this view the sages draw upon the primal image of the festive banquet. The Wisdom Woman sets the banquet table for all who will come, without money, without price, to share in the earth's blessings and to join in communion with God and with one another.

Alternative Visions of Life

Franz Kafka has said of good literature that its effect is to take an axe to the frozen sea within us.[6] From my perspective, this is true particularly of the wisdom literature. Its vision, themes and images may be able to enter our individual and collective lives, to chop away at the frozen images of death and destruction which reside there. It may be able to counter them with alternative, life-giving ways of imagining reality. It is first in the imagination that new worlds are born, there that the energy to reconceive and to remake human relationships is ignited, and there where human beings are empowered by the Spirit of their Creator.

This volume, therefore, does not provide a full commentary on any of the wisdom books. In some chapters, such as those on Job and Ecclesiastes, it does attempt a comprehensive overview of the books' purposes. Generally, however, it attempts to uncover the themes and images that might splinter the frozen sea within.

Chapter 1 introduces the world of wisdom, its terms, settings and key ideas. Chapters 2 and 3 both deal with the Book of Proverbs; the former concentrating on the older proverbial collection in cc 10-29, and the later focusing on the texts in Proverbs and elsewhere which feature the Wisdom Woman. In Chapters 4 and 5 the skeptical or "reflective" wisdom books of Job and Ecclesiastes become the subject of study. Finally, Chapters 6 and 7 address the two wisdom books not found in the Hebrew canon, but treasured by the Greek Jewish community and later by the Christian communities, the Books of Sirach and the Wisdom of Solomon.

[6]Quoted by Adolph Muschg, "Staying Alive by Learning to Write," *The New York Times Book Review,* (1 February 1987) 28.

1

WHAT IS WISDOM?

Wisdom is a fluid, mercurial term, difficult to pin down or to contain within set parameters. Throughout the biblical texts the Hebrew and Greek nouns for wisdom, *hokmah* and *sophia*, refer to broadly divergent realities: to a way of thinking, to a way of living, to a body of literature, to various technical or artistic skills, to a search for meaning and order, to sagacity about life and human relations akin to "common sense," to reverent "fear of the Lord," and, not least, to a woman, personified Wisdom herself. In its broadest sense wisdom is an approach to reality, an ethos which shares a set of ideas, assumptions and expectations about life. In the Ancient Near East, this way of thinking was international in origin and influence.

An International Way of Thinking

Though biblical scholars did not always recognize the international character of wisdom, scholars in this century uncovered a body of ancient wisdom literature. These writings cross national boundaries and bear directly upon the interpretation of the wisdom of the Bible. One of the first discoveries was the writings of an Egyptian scribe named Amen-em-opet[1] whose thirty proverbs and wise sayings exhibit

[1]"The Instruction of Amen-em-opet" in *Ancient Near Eastern Texts*, ed. James B. Pritchard (3rd edit., Princeton: Princeton University, 1969) 420-425.

strong similarities to biblical Proverbs (22:17-24:22). Subsequent discoveries revealed further parallels to biblical wisdom from Egyptian, Sumerian, Akkadian, Babylonian and Canaanite cultures.[2] As a consequence of comparative studies, it is clear that Israel's own wisdom books—Proverbs, Job, Qoheleth, the Song of Songs, Sirach and the Wisdom of Solomon— belong within a broad current of international thinking and literary production.

Wisdom as Instruction

Among the shared wisdom perspectives of the international wisdom literature was a strong didactic tone. Much of the writing was fashioned to instruct the young about proper behavior and attitudes and, thus, to prepare them for happy, successful lives. This pedagogical flavor appears particularly in collections of sayings and proverbs and in short stories.

The Eloquent Peasant

"The Protests of the Eloquent Peasant"[3] is an example of such a didactic tale from Egypt. In this account a very poor peasant sets off with the last of his goods—a mule, some bread, beer and a few remaining valuables—in search of food for his family. Along the way he meets a rich man who steals everything he has, beats him and generally terrorizes him. The peasant manages to escape from the thief and to make his way

[2]A brief and manageable discussion of Ancient Near Eastern wisdom appears in R. B. Y. Scott, *The Way of Wisdom* (New York: Macmillan, 1971) 23-48. See also Dianne Bergant, *What Are They Saying About Wisdom Literature?*, (New York: Paulist, 1984) 20-21.

[3]Pritchard, *Ancient Near Eastern Texts*, 407-410.

to a high government official before whom he pours out his complaints against the rich thief. Unbeknownst to the peasant, the official is so impressed by the eloquent wisdom spoken by the peasant that he reports the peasant's speech to the king. The king, too, becomes enthralled by the peasant's words. He orders the official to pretend not to believe the peasant. This way the peasant will keep talking and the official will be able to record his words and make a permanent record of them. Ten times the peasant pleads with the official about his circumstances. In beautiful images he argues that there is a divinely given order in the world, which the rich thief violated and which the official is obliged to set right. If only he would do so, harmony and prosperity would pervade his government, his family and his own life. Finally, the official relents. He reads back the peasant's speeches to him and he orders that the property of the rich thief be given to the eloquent peasant.

This story provides a compendium of values common to international wisdom. For example, a wise peasant is better than a rich fool. There is order and justice in the world, even if it is hidden for a time. The wise person must be patient and persevering, using speech with discipline, prudence and eloquence. Though one cannot see how and though one must wait long, prosperity and honor will come to the wise.

Didactic literature such as this functioned in the ancient world both to teach approved behavior for imitation and to teach criteria to recognize good behavior among others. These instructions were useful for coping with everyday life and for settling crises in the community. Interpreters often describe these didactic writings as optimistic in outlook because they assume that life is orderly or that it can be made orderly, even if requiring immense effort. Among the biblical didactic collection, some scholars include the story of Joseph (Gen 37;

39-47), but it is the Books of Proverbs and Sirach in which the biblical connections with international didactic literature are most apparent.

Wisdom as Skeptical Reflection

Other examples of international wisdom contrast sharply with the optimistic outlook of the "Eloquent Peasant." They express a more reflective or skeptical viewpoint on life. In these writings, the order and harmony of the world, previously presupposed, are seriously questioned, even doubted.

The Innocent Sufferer

One example of such reflective literature is the Akkadian text translated, "I will praise the Lord of Wisdom."[4] This narrative poem relates the story of a man's suffering, caused by the gods who inflict on him every kind of deprivation and pain. The man himself, however, is unable to understand why he suffers. No one "could elucidate my case," he laments, as he faces the incomprehensibility of his circumstances. Slandered by an enemy, overtaken with illness and despairing of spirit, he believes himself to be innocent and abandoned. After a time and without any explanation, he receives communications from the gods informing him that his suffering is over and that his happiness and health will be restored. Hence, he writes a poem in praise of Marduk, the Lord of Wisdom, who rescued him from his predicament.

In many ways this Mesopotamian poem parallels the story of the biblical Job, the innocent sufferer, and it asks questions

---

[4] Ibid., 596-600.

similar to those raised by Ecclesiastes and the Wisdom of Solomon. The Akkadian piece teaches that the innocent suffer because they are the victims of the whims of the gods and goddesses. Ultimately the deities restore justice and order and bring the man's suffering to an end, but their motivation appears as capricious at the end of the tale as it did at the beginning. Humans are no more than victims of unrestrained divine beings. In the reflective wisdom of the Ancient Near East, the simpler, more optimistic view of reality found in the proverbial literature disappears in a cloud of questioning and ambiguity.

A Wise Servant

A final example of Ancient Near Eastern wisdom with similarities to reflective Hebrew wisdom, particularly Ecclesiastes, is entitled, "A Pessimistic Dialogue between Master and Servant."[5] It is the story of a master who proposes to his servant ten distinct courses of action for which the master needs the servant's assistance to complete them. These include riding in a chariot, eating dinner, hunting, leading a revolution, making love to a woman. At each proposal of the master, "I will ride in a chariot," or "I will eat dinner," the servant supports his master's choice and gives additional reasons for doing the action. "Ride, Master, Ride," or "Eat, Master, Eat."

Immediately after hearing the advantages of the proposed action, the Master changes his mind. "I will not ride." Just as enthusiastically the servant supports the negative choice, "Do not ride, Master, do not ride," and supplies several reasons why the proposed course of action should be abandoned. The

[5]Ibid., 600-601.

final activity proposed by the master is to murder the servant
and to kill himself. This time the servant does not complete
the master's thought, but instead asks questions. "Who is tall
enough to ascend to heaven? Who is broad enough to embrace
the earth?" Again the master changes his mind. "No, I shall
kill you and send you ahead of me." "But Master," replies the
servant, "would you want to live even three days after me?"

One can imagine this dialogue being performed theatrically.
Written "tongue in cheek," it sets before the readers a riddle or
a paradox. Life is ambiguous. Good and bad consequences
result from every human activity. The reader is teased and
amused at the obsequious agreeableness of the servant and
outwitted by him in the end. The whole piece is a joke to
provoke laughter and deep reflection about the complexity of
life. Similarly, the biblical Ecclesiastes respects life's ambiguity
and probes the opaqueness of the world for meaning and order
and, I will argue, with deliberate and puzzling mirth.

Even this small sampling of Ancient Near Eastern wisdom
reveals a wide variety of approaches to the common concern of
wisdom thinkers—human experience. From the perceptions
which they shared with their neighbors, the sages of Israel
drew language and ideas to express their own conceptual
world, at once both international and specific in character.
Consequently, the international writings offer clues for approaching specific biblical books and for assessing how they
both agreed with and differed from those of their neighbors. It
is in the context of these international human concerns and
perennial human dilemmas that Israel articulates its particular
experience of faith. Eventually, wisdom thinking will provide
Israel with unique insights into its relationship with its God.

Solomon, The Exemplar of Israelite Wisdom

In Israel one figure, Solomon the great king and patron of wisdom, came to exemplify many facets of the wisdom traditions. According to 1 Kings 3-11 Solomon was renowned for his wisdom in the ancient world. When he inherited the throne of Israel from his father David, Solomon asked God for the gift of wisdom and he received it.

> "I give you a wise and discerning mind so that none like you has been before and none like you will arise after you. I give you also what you have not asked, both riches and honor so that no other King will compare with you" (1 K 3:12-13).

Much of the remainder of cc 3-11 illustrates the effects of the divine wisdom upon Solomon and his rule. For example, immediately following Solomon's dialogue with God is the familiar story of Solomon's wise judgement (1 K 3:16-25). This account demonstrates his keen discernment, his understanding of human nature and his clever maneuvering through a dilemma that contributed to his reputation as the wisest man.

Two women are arguing over the identity of the mother of one living baby (1 K 3:16-25).

"I am the mother!"

"No, I am the mother!"

At this apparent impasse, Solomon orders the soldiers to slice the baby in two and give half to each woman. One woman agrees to the solution rather than relinquish her claim upon the child; the other gives up her claim so that the child might live. Thus Solomon discovers which of the women is truly concerned to give life to the child.

Another incident that reveals Solomon's wisdom was the

visit paid him by the Queen of Sheba. Sheba was itself a place known for its wisdom, so when the Queen came to Jerusalem she was well able to testify that Solomon's wisdom surpassed her expectations (1 K 10:6). To her the principal evidence of Solomon's wisdom was his immense wealth. Typically the people of the ancient world saw the possession of wealth as a material sign of God's blessing. Hence, the wise were expected to be wealthy, and the wealthy were perceived as wise.

However, Solomon's wisdom extended beyond his wealth to other qualities which provide further clues about wisdom in Israel. In Solomon's case, wisdom included the gifts necessary for ruling a nation with discernment, great knowledge and largeness of mind (1 K 4:29). It referred to the talents to memorize and to create proverbial sayings and wisdom songs (4:32). Moreover, that Solomon was wise meant that he had the ability to categorize the names of trees, beasts, birds, reptiles and fish, that is, have extensive knowledge of the science of the natural world as it was known among the ancients. But perhaps Solomon's wisest act was the establishment of a court in Jerusalem where he gathered about him scribes and learned people to aid him in his pursuits (1 K 4:1-6), and thus to promote the spread of wisdom.[6]

Though other biblical texts take a less glorious view of his achievements (for example, 1 K 11:1-9), it is clear that Solomon was a great hero in wisdom circles. His name is associated with four wisdom books: Proverbs, Ecclesiastes, the Song of Songs and the Wisdom of Solomon. Because these writings span a period of time from the ninth century to the

---

[6]Walter Brueggemann, *(In Man We Trust: The Neglected Side of Biblical Faith,* Atlanta: John Knox, 1972) claims an important historical role in the establishment of wisdom circles for David, Solomon's predecessor.

first, his authorship of all of them, perhaps any of them, is impossible. However, in a world where authorship was ascribed to a great figure of the past to bring authority to the work, the use of his name reveals his legendary stature among Israel's sages. As a wisdom figure Solomon encapsulates many aspects of the wisdom tradition, as if his portrait were embellished to make him wisdom's representative.

Wisdom as Knowledge

The example of Solomon indicates that wisdom in Israel involved the pursuit of knowledge. The modern adage that knowledge is power would probably have been accepted by Israel's wisdom thinkers, though they would understand both knowledge and power differently. In the ancient world knowledge was not something that was separate from ordinary experience, but flowed from it and illuminated it. The notion that knowledge placed its possessors in an "ivory tower," aloof and uninvolved with the world, would have been impossible for a people who saw the world and the human being as unities. For them the human person was an organic whole so that thinking and knowing were integral to living. All knowledge, therefore, was directly useful in helping one to understand the created world and to cope with human existence. The more one knew, the better one would be able to live.

Hakam, the Hebrew adjective meaning "wise," referred to persons possessing a variety of forms of knowledge. In addition to knowing specific skills such as shipbuilding (Ps 107:27), the wise were those with detailed information regarding the physical world, or they were the creators and transmitters of proverbs and wise sayings, crystallizing the knowledge of the community. In its deepest sense, of course, the wise referred to those who had a profound understanding of human existence in every dimension and especially human relationship with God. Hence, wisdom involved knowledge, often intuitively or experientially gained, which could be transmitted to the next generation. To distinguish wisdom from other Old Testament traditions (like prophetic and covenant traditions),R. N. Whybray, calls wisdom an intellectual tradition.[7] It is produced by individuals in every generation who thought about life's deepest questions and passed their thought onto others.

The Transmission of Wisdom—Folk Wisdom

Over many centuries the accumulated wisdom of the people grew into a body of knowledge which was preserved orally and passed on from parents to children. The wisdom heritage of Israel, therefore, was the product, at least in part, of the common people. Often called folk or clan wisdom, it was created and transmitted by them. It lived among them as a guide to daily life, as a way to educate younger members of the community and as a resource for settling conflicts among them.

In many parts of the world today among various cultures and ethnic groups, and in particular, among the tribal cultures of Africa and among the indigenous peoples of Latin America, the same process continues. These communities use the treasure of their proverbial wisdom to establish their collective identity and to conduct their lives according to the distilled experience of their ancestors.

---

[7] *The Intellectual Tradition in the Old Testament* (Berlin: Walter de Gruyter, 1974).

Professional Wisdom

However in the Ancient Near East wisdom was not the exclusive property of the folk or clan. The *hakam*, the wise, also included the professionals, the sages, who were experts in knowledge of one sort or another. Eventually a class of professional sages arose across the ancient world. Kings and rulers gathered these learned citizens around them as advisors and courtiers. The royal courts supported and encouraged the sages as a literate class. Because diplomatic contacts with other nations was a normal part of court life, it was probably among the court sages that wisdom thinking spread from one culture to another.

In Israel it was probably among them that the sayings of the folk were collected, recorded, and embellished by the sages' own polished additions. Furthermore, it was probably this professional class of sages, whether in the court or not, who expanded the wisdom repertoire to include long didactic tales and more reflective writings that probe the deeper questions of human life. It would have been they who collected, edited or created Israel's wisdom masterpieces.[8]

Wisdom as Intelligence

Though wisdom involves knowledge, it cannot be described exclusively as knowledge, or perhaps not even primarily as knowledge. Wisdom also includes a basic, earthy intelligence

[8]For discussions of the controversies regarding the role of court sages see Roland E. Murphy, "Wisdom—Theses and Hypotheses" in *Israelite Wisdom: Theological and Literary Essays in Honor of Samuel Terrien*, ed. John G. Gammie, et al. (New York: Union Theological Seminary, 1978) 35-42; James L. Crenshaw, *Old Testament Wisdom* (Atlanta: John Knox, 1981) 28-39; and Whybray, *The Intellectual Tradition*, 15-54.

that enables the one with knowledge to use it effectively. Wisdom requires the judgment, the skills, and the prudence to interpret different situations and to cope with them successfully. Because life is everchanging, and because few circumstances repeat themselves exactly, the wise are the ones with the vigilance, flexibility and right thinking to meet life in all its contingencies with grace, compassion and understanding.

Wisdom as Gift

Ultimately, biblical wisdom is neither innate talent nor disciplined human achievement; it is divine gift. Wisdom is something, or rather someone, to be sought after, to pursue, to pray for, but finally, it is Wisdom who finds us.

2

HOW TO COPE WITH LIFE

In chapters 10-39, the Book of Proverbs contains several collections of short sayings or proverbs. Though attributed to Solomon and other sages, the proverbs come from a variety of circumstances and times in Israel's history. A prologue of nine chapters (cc 1-9) written some time after the Exile now introduces the older proverbial collections. Chapters 30-31 are also later additions to the Book.[1] This chapter will discuss themes of cc 10-29. The next chapter will consider poems from cc 1-9 and c 31.

The Authors

No single author is responsible for all the sayings in cc 10-31 of the Book of Proverbs. Solomon is credited with authorship of many of them (10:1; 22:17; 25:1). However, Agur (30:1) and Lemuel (31:1) are named in the last part of the Book, and two other sections are identified as "The Sayings of the Wise" (22:17[2] and 24:23). Often in the ancient world, a

[1]For a brief discussion of the additions to the collected sayings, see R. B. Y. Scott, *Proverbs, Ecclesiastes*, Anchor Bible 18 (Garden City: Doubleday, 1965) 15-22.

[2]Scholars have long recognized close similarities between "the words of the wise" of Provs 22:17-24:22 and the Egyptian writing, "The Instruction of

venerable figure, not the actual writer, was named as author to bring authority to the work. The sayings are the utterances of parents, heads of clans or elders, scribes of the kings' courts, religious leaders and wise teachers, called sages. At the end of long periods of oral transmission, the sages collected the sayings, preserved them, added to them and arranged them in the Book of Proverbs. Proverbial wisdom, then, is the collected wisdom of the people. It grew out of the daily lives, relationships and struggles of educated and of uneducated, of noble and of ordinary folk.

Word Pictures

Proverbs is like a collection of word pictures or verbal snapshots. Unclassified and generally lacking in thematic or chronological order, the collected sayings resemble a family's cache of photos, placed randomly in a drawer year after year till rememberance of relationships among them is lost. These word pictures reveal the wise and the foolish in action.[3] They are captured in typical moments of thought and behavior, which, as a collection of moments, illustrate wise and foolish orientations toward all of life. In the life of the community, these word pictures or collected sayings serve several purposes.

The Purposes of Proverbs

One purpose of Proverbs is surely to entertain. A quick survey of a few chapters presents the reader with glimpses of

Amen-em-opet." The later text is available in James B. Pritchard, ed., *Ancient Near Eastern Texts* (Princeton: Princeton University, 1969) 421-425.

[3]Robert Alter, (*The Art of Biblical Poetry*, New York: Basic Books, 1985, 163-184), speaks about the "narrativity" of proverbs.

humanity in all its foibles, its wickedness and its charm. In many ways human behavior hardly seems to have changed over the centuries. Consider this saying, for instance. "The one who blesses his neighbor with a loud voice, getting up early in the morning, will be counted as cursing" (27:14. My translation). Anyone awakened too early by someone's friendly intentions can laugh at the truth of this observation. The deeper point of the proverb, however, is that timing is everything. Good intentions acted upon at the wrong moment can produce terrible results.

A broader purpose of Proverbs is to instruct the young, the "simple," the unsophisticated, in the life of wisdom. The Book does this, not by issuing commands or articulating doctrine, but by comparing the good with the bad, the wise with the foolish. One of the meanings of *mashal*,[4] the Hebrew word for proverb, is "to compare."[5] The word pictures compare models of wise living which is to be emulated, with examples of foolish behavior which is to be avoided. These comparisons inspire, encourage and challenge all members of the com-

[4]The literary type of the *mashal* includes more than proverbs. Folk tales, similitudes, fables, parables, taunt songs and other forms of comparative and metaphorical literature are classified this way. For discussion of the *mashal* see: James L. Crenshaw, "Wisdom" in *Old Testament Form Criticism*, John L. Hayes, ed., Trinity University, Monograph Series in Religion, (San Antonio: Trinity University, 1974) 229-239; and George M. Landes, "Jonah: A. Masal?" in *Wisdom: Theological and Literary Essays in Honor or Samuel Terrien*, John G. Gammie, et al, eds. (Scholars Press; New York: Union Theological Seminary, 1978) 137-158.

[5]Sometimes the second element in the comparison is the opposite of the first, sometimes an extension or an embellishment of the first, and at still other times, the comparison is merely implied in the proverb. Various types of proverbs are described in Dermot Cox, *Proverbs*, Old Testament Message (Wilmington: Michael Glazier, 1982) 84-89; James L.Crenshaw, *Old Testament Wisdom: An Introduction*

munity to live virtuously, to live fully, that is, to enter "the goodness of life."[6]

Since for Israel, wisdom is a force already present in the world, to teach virtue is to enable the individual to enter into and to collaborate with this force of goodness and harmony which surrounds them. Virtuous living, therefore, is cooperation with wisdom; foolish living, its rejection.

Proverbs makes no attempt to systematize this instruction or to convey principles of behavior or morality. Instead, the Book depicts the wise and the foolish in action in real situations, in the family, in business and in community life. Thus concrete models of wise and foolish behavior create a resource for individuals to appropriate and apply to their own circumstances.

Another purpose of Proverbs is to enable the individual to cope with or "to rule over" the chaos of life. A second root meaning of *mashal*, the Hebrew word for proverb, is "to rule over." By possessing the right proverb and applying it to an ambiguous or confusing situation, the individual can interpret the event and choose the correct response.[7] For example, when trying to decide whether or not to get involved in someone else's argument, this proverb might help: "Like catching a stray dog by the ear, so is meddling in the quarrels of others" (26:17. My translation). "Keep out!" this saying advises. From

(Atlanta: John Knox, 1981) 67-72; and the very readable summary by Roland E. Murphy, *Wisdom Literature and the Psalms*, Interpreting Biblical Texts (Nashville: Abingdon, 1983) 37-42.

[6]An expression of Dermot Cox, *Proverbs*, 58-66.

[7]Carole R. Fontaine demonstrates this function of the proverb, what she calls "proverb performance," in her study *Traditional Sayings in the Old Testament: A Contextual Study*, Bible and Literature Series (Sheffield: Almond Press, 1982).

another vantage point, a wise person could use the same proverb as a warning to prevent others from meddling in her argument. Should they dare, they can expect to be bitten.

In such circumstances proverbs give their possessors insight into the situation, and they give them the ability to choose their own actions and to influence the actions of others. Proverbs empower the wise to "rule over" the chaos of life. Underlying this function of the sayings is the belief that, though present in the world, wisdom is often hidden. On the surface of things, life is chaotic and unclear. A suitable proverb can bring light to the darkness and it can empower its bearer to make a safe path through danger.

The Mode of Instruction

Another meaning of *mashal*, or proverb is "riddle" or "puzzle." In furnishing the wise with comparisons, the sayings often create puzzles or riddles that require reflection to uncover their secrets. Though there are a variety of proverbial types in the Book, most of the sayings cloak the point of the comparison in hints and allusions rather than state it explicitly. To gain a synthesis between the two elements compared requires an engagement of the hearer's imagination, a puzzling out of the insights implied in the comparison. For example, "With patience a ruler may be persuaded, and a soft tongue will break a bone" (25:15). In both elements of the comparison, gentle or restrained behavior triumphs over the more powerful reality. But this insight is not explicitly stated. It must be deduced by the listener or reader. Implied in this method of teaching is a perception of the freedom of the human being and of the ambiguous nature of life.

The Choice

Proverbial wisdom assumes that people are capable of choosing, are free to choose, indeed, must choose their own course of action in life. The reason for this emphasis is that life is ambiguous and multivalent. No predetermined recipe, blueprint or teaching can prepare one for all the turns and permutations of life. Though some of the proverbs are quite dogmatic and prescriptive in tone, appearing to contradict this claim, few teach behaviors that are universally applicable. Instead, each word photo captures a virtue or a behavior appropriate for a particular moment, or an attitude that is generally desirable, but not universally so.

Moreover, for every simple, clear statement of how one should act, there is another simple, clear statement demanding its opposite. For example, "Do not speak harshly"; and its opposite, "do not refrain from rebuking." Or, "Wealth is great security"; and its modification, "a good name is better than wealth." "Never lend money"; but, "to the poor, lend." To obey every saying would produce schizophrenia. What is sought is not blind acceptance of any proverb, but the flexibility of mind to determine what behavior is appropriate for each situation. Because life is ambiguous and mysterious, Proverbs calls forth creative responses for each new circumstance. To cope with life wisely means to make wise choices.

The choice to become wise is not a single decision, made and then forgotten. It is a lifetime of choices, an orientation of one's entire being. In Proverbs, wisdom is a spirituality, an enduring stance toward life which incorporates a broad range of chosen attitudes and behaviors, often called virtues. These virtues appear only as glimpses, single moments integral to an entire way of life. They are not to be imitated in a rigid way or in isolation from one another, but are to be integrated into the whole person's thinking and acting. In contemporary language, a person possessing the virtues of the wise would be called mature, whole, a full human being able to love and to be loved. To possess the virtues of the wise is to live deeply and intensely, in rich relationships with all of life and, ultimately, with God. The following are typical virtues of the wise.

THE QUALITIES OF THE WISE

Humility

In the collected sayings, wisdom's prerequisite is humility. To become wise individuals must have open minds; they must be able to stand before life and to learn from it. Some people are incapable of learning, not because they lack intelligence, but because they lack humility. Moreover, such people disrupt the community because they are unable to learn from others. "By insolence the heedless make strife, but with those who take advice is wisdom" (13:10). The humble, on the other hand, are those who are aware that there is more to life than their limited experience of it. They can recognize the narrowness of their own frame of reference, and so they are teachable. Conversely, people without humility join the ranks of the fools and suffer the consequences. "The wise of heart will heed commandments, but a prating fool will come to ruin" (10:8).

For the humble, life is a search for the truth which must be pursued continuously in the changing circumstances of human existence. "Do not boast about tomorrow, for you do not know what a day may bring forth" (27:1). Since, for the humble, there are still things to be learned, humility encourages a dynamic relationship to life and to other people. This idea is put negatively and then positively in this saying, "A fool despises his father's instruction, but the one who heeds admonition is prudent" (15:5). Moreover, humility is desirable for practical reasons. "Pride will being a person low, but the one who is lowly in spirit will obtain honor" (29:23 my translation). Finally, humility is paired with the greatest virtue of the wise, the fear of Yahweh, in gaining benefits for its possessor. "The reward for humility and fear of the Lord is riches and honor and life" (22:4).

Diligence

Another trait of the wise is diligence. Fundamental to this virtue is the willingness to channel energy into one's responsibilities. The diligent persevere single-mindedly, like the oxen. "Where there are no oxen, there is no grain; but abundant crops come by the strength of the ox" (14:4). In this proverb, results come from trudging, constant work. The image of the oxen plowing the field or threshing the grain evokes ideas of steadiness, dependability and straining effort. The wise person works like an ox.

The opposite of diligence is laziness. "A slack hand causes

poverty, but the hand of the diligent makes rich" (10:4). While laziness produces a life of poverty and want, diligence yields prosperity. In the world of wisdom where cause and effect are organically joined, timely, persistent hard work inevitably gives birth to wealth and power. "The hand of the diligent will rule, while the slothful will be put to forced labor" (12:24).

Diligence extends to all of life's endeavors, even parenting. The one who spares the rod hates the child; but the one who loves him is diligent to discipline him" (13:24 my translation). According to this well-known proverb, watchful tending of children is the mark of diligent and responsible parents. In another saying, diligence stretches beyond the notion of faithful hard work to include the idea of prudent judgment. "The plans of the diligent lead surely to abundance, but every one who is hasty comes only to want" (21:5). This proverb compares wealth that comes from thoughtful planning with the want that comes from hasty or careless actions. It was a common belief of the community that diligent concentration and industrious labor would enable one to escape the plight of the poverty-stricken fool.

Prudence

As important as it is, however, diligence must be balanced by other human qualities. By itself, diligence may not even be useful. Too easily one might apply it to the wrong things. Treated in isolation from the whole person and life's concrete situations, virtues degenerate into obsessions. Like every human activity, diligence is valuable only when governed by prudence. Prudence is the guiding intelligence which dictates what action or withdrawal from action is appropriate in a specific situation.

Learning prudence is like learning to cook. The art of cooking can be acquired only by experience. Some basic steps can be applied generally, but the production of a good meal requires practiced discernment. When an ingredient is missing from one's pantry, what can be substituted? When the dinner crowd suddenly increases, what amount of new ingredients must be added? If the sauce thickens too much or not enough, if things brown too quickly, if the oven refuses to heat evenly, how does one adjust the temperature and the timing to achieve the desired results? And most difficult of all, how are things to be managed so that they all finish cooking at the same time? The skilled cook performs miracles almost effortlessly, through habitual responses learned from years of experience, advice and experimentation. Similarly, prudent people apply such experience-honed judgment to every corner of life.

"The wisdom of the prudent is to discern his way" (14:8a). The prudent know when to act and when to resist action. "The prudent person sees danger and hides, but the simple go on and suffer for it" (27:12 my translation). Likewise, "The vexation of the fool is known at once, but the prudent one forgives an insult" (12:16 my translation). Prudence is the essential mark of the wise person because life is often ambiguous, confusing and opaque to interpretation. Though wisdom permeates the universe, it is mysteriously hidden. To recognize wisdom, to distinguish it from false values posing as good, to interpret the events around them, the wise need the discerning judgment called prudence.

Prudence enables the wise to distinguish between the relative values of two apparently good results. "A good name is to be chosen rather than great riches, and favor is better than silver or gold" (22:1). According to this saying, both name and riches do one good, but the former is, in the end, of higher value in community life. Similar calculating judgment permits the selection of reliable allies in work. "He who sends a message by the hand of a fool cuts off his own feet and drinks violence" (26:6).

Prudence in Speaking

The Book of Proverbs attends particularly to prudent use of the tongue. The large number of sayings concerned with aspects of speech (over sixty) convey the impression that careless or vicious speech was a major problem in ancient Israel. However, the recognition that speaking was the only form of communication available to most people in the ancient world helps to place these sayings in perspective.

In many communities no one was able to read or write. Public and private business had to be conducted by word of mouth because no other medium of communication was available. Legal proceedings rested heavily on the reliability of the speech of the witnesses. In contrast, today's instant and retrievable communication makes of speech a ghost of its previous incarnations. In western society it is often uttered carelessly, credited with little power, and no one need remember it. In oral societies the opposite is true. What one says is remembered, and the spoken word profoundly affects the life of the community. As a result, a person's speech must be utterly reliable, and it must be appropriate to the occasion for which it is uttered. It is these skills which enable the wise to use proverbs effectively and, thus, to "rule over" those situations in life which require insightful interpretation.

To encourage proper speech, Proverbs instructs the wise in its power. The mouth of the wise is a "fountain of life" (10:11a); "on the lips of the one who has understanding, wisdom is found" (10:13a); "the tongue of the righteous is choice silver" (10:20a); "the lips of the righteous feed many" (10:21a), and "the lips of the righteous know what is acceptable" (10:32a); "a gentle tongue is a tree of life" (15:4a); "pleasant words are like honeycomb; sweetness to the soul and health to the body" (16:24). Even rebuking words can be life-giving to the community: "A bold rebuke makes peace" (10:10b my translation).

However, like everything in the proverbial battery of virtues, there is a reverse side to the power of speech. Evil words bring death. For example, "Perverseness in it (the tongue) breaks the spirit" (15:4b). "The mouth of the wicked conceals violence" (10:11b). "The one who covers over hatred has lying lips, and the one who utters slander is a fool" (10:18 my translation). However, silence is not always a better choice. Though false speech can harm the community, "Better is open rebuke than hidden love" (27:5). Prudent timing is the secret of wise speech. "A word fitly spoke is like apples of gold in a setting of silver" (25:11).

Proverbs teaches vigilant discipline in the communication process which was so vital for social existence. As a speaker, one must be on guard to discern when and if to speak. "Even a fool who keeps silent is considered wise; when he closes his lips, he is deemed intelligent" (17:28). If speaking is the prudent choice, then one must suit words to the occasion, sometimes pleasant words, sometimes angry words. As a listener, one must distinguish between the words of the wise and the words of the fool. Prudence in this regard is not a simple matter, but it can be learned. "In everything a prudent person acts with knowledge, but a fool parades his folly" (13:16 my translation).

Self-Mastery

In the extended families of ancient Israel emotional outbursts of any kind were potentially destructive of family and community harmony. Consequently, wise living was disciplined living. Though Proverbs extends discipline to many facets of daily life, a number of sayings concentrate on the control of anger. Since wrongly or violently expressed anger was particularly perilous for the community, the wise bridle their anger. "A hot-headed person provokes strife, but the one who is slow to anger quiets contention" (15:18 my translation). Angry people can be troublesome to everyone, including themselves. "A man of great wrath will pay the penalty, for if you deliver him, you will only have to do it again" (19:19).

There are also practical reasons for controlling anger. Besides being destructive of the community, the habit of angry outbursts damages one's reputation as a person of intelligence and discipline. Furthermore, inappropriate expressions of ire might provoke the wrath of others more powerful than oneself, like the King, resulting in the forfeit of one's life (20:2), hardly worth it to feel better for a moment. Though unprovoked or violent anger reveals a person out of control, anger is not considered bad in itself. It is to be examined slowly, weighed, and only when appropriate, acted upon. "Better be slow to anger than a fighter, better rule over the spirit than capture a city" (16:32 my translation).

The sayings about anger teach that discipline is essential to wise living, but they may have had other uses in the community. One can imagine them being used to diffuse the power of someone's anger. For example, to respond to a furious person with the remark that, "A fool comes out with all anger, but the wise one holds it back" (29:11 my translation), would undercut the force of that anger, discrediting it as the expression of a fool. But if the angry person reminds the community that "The one who reproves another will afterward find more favor than the one who flatters with the tongue" (28:23 my translation), her anger may gain a hearing. Like all the qualities of the wise, self-mastery is useful only when practiced in a balanced fashion and in an appropriate way.

Integrity

Without self-mastery a person is not yet a person. Proverbs describes someone lacking it in this way: "A city broken into and left without walls is a person without control of his spirit" (25:28). In the ancient world, a city without walls is a city wasted, without protection or identity. This saying describes a human without a center, a distracted and unfocused being, unable to love others because there is no integrity within.

People lacking integrity are parched at the core of their beings. "Like clouds and wind without rain, is one who boasts of a gift he does not have" (25:14). Or, "Like a muddied spring or a polluted fountain is a righteous person who gives way to the wicked" (25:26 my translation). Both of these sayings speak of nature gone awry—a cloud that fails to produce rain, water that destroys rather than nourishes. Similarly, human beings without integrity are unable to function in relationships with others. They fail to nourish and they can destroy the life of the community. In the most severe cases, they are pitiable beings.

The actions of people of integrity are consonant with their inner lives. They are people of *shalom* or wholeness. In Hebrew, the word for "integrity" *tom*, also means "wholeness" or "completeness." When applied to people it conveys a sense of honesty and self-possession, or as we would say, maturity. Such people seem to live from within, fed by inner springs known only to them. They have a profound honesty about themselves and the world, and they have the self-possession to act accordingly. Such people are particularly secure, perhaps because they have nothing to hide and, ultimately, nothing to lose. "The one who walks in integrity walks in safety" (10:9 my translation). Because of these qualities, people of integrity are able to be responsible and loyal in human relationships, the arena wherein all the virtues of the wise are employed.

Fidelity in Relationships

The harmonious relationships of the wise with their families, friends and even their enemies both creates and reveals the order and harmony of the universe. In the Book of Proverbs, loyalty to the family, particularly to one's parents, is of central importance. This is stated negatively. "He who does violence to his father and he chases away his mother is a son who causes shame and brings reproach" (19:26). Similarly, "He who robs his father or his mother and says, 'That is not transgression,' is the companion of a man who destroys" (28:24).

Beyond parental relationships, the wise actively work to create harmony among siblings, if that is what the term "brother" means in the following proverb. "A brother helped is like a strong city, but quarreling is like the bars of a castle" (18:19). To aid anyone in the family strengthens the whole social unit against outside attacks; to quarrel creates barriers within, dissolving the family's resilience to attack.

Fidelity is not limited to the family. "A friend loves at all times and a brother is born for adversity" (17:17). This saying exhorts the individual to be a loyal friend, and it also encourages her to make faithful friends for her own times of adversity. Though the quality of friendship is tested in adversity, one should be wary, for fidelity is rare even among friends. "Many people proclaim themselves loyal, but a faithful friend who can find?" (20:6 my translation). As parents have always insisted, friends must be selected with great caution. "Never make friends with an angry person nor go with a wrathful person" (22:24 my translation).

Neighbors, too, deserve proper treatment, sometimes consisting of omission rather than commission. "Let your foot be seldom in your neighbor's house, lest he become weary of you and hate you" (25:17). And, "Be not a witness against your neighbor without cause" (24:28a). Both of these proverbs describe actions, one annoying, the other, vicious, which can ruin connections among neighbors.

Even in the treatment of enemies where bonds of fidelity are not at stake, the wise act with restraint. For instance, "Do not say I will do to him as he has done to me; I will pay back the man for what he has done" (24:29). To gloat over the enemy's doom can be a greater offense against God than the original wickedness of the enemy. "Do not rejoice when your enemy falls and let your heart be glad when he stumbles; lest the Lord see it and be displeased, and turn his anger away from him" (24:17-18). This saying appeals to God to encourage restraint within society, and it offers a divine warrant for respectful behavior in all human dealings.

Wisdom is Relational

The spirituality of Proverbs is a relational one. Though the sayings portray one virtue and then another, the intention is holistic; the virtues or qualities of the wise concern the whole person and affect the entire community. Because Israel was a community-oriented culture, the goal of the sayings was to perfect the community, not just the individual. Unlike North American culture where the well-being of the individual holds the highest importance, in community-oriented cultures,[8] the good of the family, the clan, the village is the highest value. As a result, the virtues taught in Proverbs have a social focus. What really matters, according to Proverbs, is the way one relates to the community. Relationships make life beautiful, challenge people at the core of their beings, and provide the most intense and surprising joy.

Proper, respectful and wise relationships with others is the matrix of wisdom in the Book of Proverbs. Though some may appear to focus on personal enhancement, all the qualities of the wise are directed toward peaceful, life-giving relationships in the society. The sayings directed specifically to relationships simply make explicit what is implicit elsewhere. Proverbial wisdom presents an other-directed stance toward life as the essence of wisdom. Religious practices, prayer, formal worship have little place in its vision. To live intensely and to cope

[8]In this respect, ancient Israelite culture is not unlike the Chinese, Japanese and African community-oriented cultures of today.

successfully with life's dilemmas, live honestly, faithfully, encouraging and enhancing the lives of others. This will make one happy, secure and blessed; any other course will lead to misery.

The Fear of Yahweh

Proper relationship of the individual with God is not a major issue in early wisdom sayings, but neither is it completely neglected. Rather, in its use of the expression "fear of Yahweh," Proverbs assumes that authentic relationship with God informs and guides the wise. This assumption is made explicit in the introduction to Proverbs where fear of Yahweh "is the beginning of knowledge" (1:7a). In the collected sayings, however, the expression is used frequently, though never explained. Explanation is unnecessary because the phrase was a well known formula in Israel.[9]

Among the many meanings associated with fear of Yahweh, terror or fright are not included. The fear of Yahweh is a relational term which refers to overpowering awe and wonder, combined with powerful attraction humans experience in the presence of the Living God. True fear of Yahweh is expressed in loving trustful obedience. "The one who walks in uprightness fears Yahweh" (14:2a my translation). Fear of Yahweh gives one a sense of right and wrong, motivated neither from terror nor from a legal purity, but by intimate relationship with the God of justice and harmony.[10] Moreover, fear of Yahweh gives confidence and security. "In the fear of Yahweh

9"Fear of Yahweh" is discussed in Cox, *Proverbs*, 67-71; and in Gerhard von Rad, *Wisdom in Israel* (Nashville: Abingdon, 1972) 66-73.

10Cox, *Proverbs*, 67-71.

one has strong confidence and his children will have a refuge"
(14:26).

To live in the fear of Yahweh is to live in loving devotion, in
close relationship, which makes humans feel small before such
a being. Only those who have entered this relationship can
recognize the wisdom and harmony pulsing through the
universe. The fear of Yahweh is the summary virtue of the
sages. "The fear of the Lord is instruction in wisdom and
humility goes before honor" (15:33). Those who possess it are
enlightened people, able to recognize the wisdom which has
always embraced them. In the end, they receive wisdom as a
gift of God and they live conscious of their integral oneness
with all of God's creation.

Moral Gleanings Regarding Wealth and Poverty

Proverbs does not teach a morality or an ethics in a
thorough or systematic way. But because it is relational,
Proverbs teaches an ethical stance towards life. It presents
moral gleanings, ethical hints of a moral vision which is highly
respectful of all human beings. An apparent exception to this
claim are the numerous sayings about the poor and the rich.
Because the relationship of the rich and the poor is a major
ethical question of our time, these sayings are of particular
concern. To place them in context, it may be helpful to
consider Israel's attitudes toward wealth and poverty.

Regarding the poor, Proverbs appears cruel and heartless.
Some proverbs deride the poor as lazy and worthless. "The
sluggard bruises his hand in the dish, and will not even bring it
back to his mouth" (19:24). Furthermore, the victims are
blamed for their victimhood. "Slothfulness casts into a deep
sleep, and an idle person suffers hunger" (19:15). In several

sayings, the poor are depicted as choosing hunger. "He who tills his land will have plenty of bread, but he who follows worthless pursuits will have plenty of poverty" (28:19).

The formula is quite simple. Hard work brings profit; laziness brings poverty. According to this view, wise living is automatically accompanied by material blessing. This means that material well-being is largely the result of individual effort. "In all toil there is profit, but mere talk tends only to want" (14:23). Even more explicitly, God rewards wisdom. "The reward for humility and fear of the Lord is riches and honor and life" (22:4).

However, these ancient teachings are not as crassly mercenary as they first appear. In the unitary view of the world held by the ancients, action and result are organically connected. Choice sets in motion an immediate cause and effect relationship between the choice and the result. Good actions bring forth good results and bad actions yield evil results. This is why, for them, hard work brings blessing. One good produces another good. Furthermore, doing good and receiving good are signs that one has collaborated with the forces of wisdom already present in the world.[11]

In addition, the economic conditions of ancient Israel contributed to its appreciation of wealth. The economic system could propel whole families into ruin, jeopardizing even physical survival. Borrowing and lending were completely uncontrolled. Any interest could be charged and loans could be called in at the lender's whim. Drought, plague, or war could send families into an escalating cycle of debt, leaving them no recourse but to sell off ancestral property or to sell themselves into slavery to meet the incorrigible demands of

[11]Von Rad, *Wisdom*, 77-96.

lenders. Under these circumstances, the avoidance of poverty meant, ultimately, the avoidance of degradation and death.[12]

Then as now, wealth was highly valued because it gave security and stability in the face of the unexpected in life. "A rich man's wealth is his strong city, and like a high wall protecting him" (18:11). Since wealth meant security, Proverbs urges the wise to work for it unceasingly. "Love not sleep, lest you come to poverty; open your eyes and you will have plenty of bread" (20:13). Save for the future. "Precious treasure remains in a wise person's dwelling, but the foolish devour it" (21:20 my translation). Do not lend money imprudently for everything might be lost. "He who gives surety for a stranger will smart for it, but he who hates suretyship is secure" (11:15).

Because wealth enabled families to keep the wolf away from the door, I believe that the negative statements about the poor in Proverbs serve a pedagogical purpose. They are not teachings about the character of the poor. Their purpose is to exhort the young to do everything within their power to avoid poverty by working diligently and by being vigilant for opportunity. Furthermore, they serve as a warning that prudence, vigilance and effort are absolutely necessary for survival.

This interpretation is supported by the fact that Proverbs presents an alternative portrait of the poor. Only the most callous believe that the poor deserve to be poor, that they live in deprivation because they are sluggards, cheats, no goods. The opinion, often heard today, that the poor choose poverty because they lack goals, drive and basic human goodness has

---

[12]Willy Schrottroff ("The Prophet Amos: A Socio-Historical Assessment of His Ministry" in *God of the Lowly: Socio-Historical Interpretations of the Bible*, Willy Schottroff and Wolfgang Stegemann, eds.; Maryknoll: Orbis, 1984, 27-46), details the economic situation in eighth century Israel.

never been true. It may be true of some of the poor, but these character slurs also apply to some of the wealthy.

Proverbs recognizes this fact. Some of the sayings speak sympathetically about the poor. The poor are not all fools; they can be wise people who contradict the arrogance of the rich and powerful. "Wise in his own eyes is a rich man, but a poor person of understanding will find him out" (28:11 my translation). Moreover, some proverbs observe that the poor are trapped in their circumstances. "The ransom of a man's life is his wealth, but a poor man has no means of redemption" (13:8). In ancient Israel, when poverty forced the sale of family property or the sale of family members into slavery, the law provided for the repurchase of the land or the people by a relative called a "redeemer." This is the original meaning of the biblical concept of redemption. However, the poor, then as now, were often situated in a cycle of poverty in which kinfolk were equally destitute and unable to rescue them.

Besides the sayings that are respectful of the poor, a great number of sayings exhort the rich to share their wealth. "All day long the wicked covets, but the righteous give and do not hold back" (21:26). Moreover, wealth wrongly acquired, will ultimately be given to the generous. "He who augments wealth by interest and increase gathers it for him who is kind to the poor" (28:8).

A number of proverbs provide enticing motivation for caring for the poor. They assert that generosity is double-edged. It is for the good of the other, but it will redound to the good of the giver. "One person gives freely, yet grows richer, another is stingy and only suffers want" (11:24 my translation). "A liberal man will be enriched, and one who waters will in turn be watered" (11:25); "He who has a bountiful eye will be blessed, for he shares bread with the poor" (22:9);

"The one who gives to the poor will not want, but the one who covers the eyes will get many curses" (28:27 my translation). The reverse is also true. "He who closes his ear to the cry of the poor will himself cry out and not be heard" (21:13).

However, true motivation for generosity to the poor arises from more than the boomerang effect generosity sets in motion. Proverbs insists that the poor and the rich are equal before God; they are connected as sisters and brothers before the one Creator. "The rich and the poor meet together; the Lord is the maker of them all" (22:2). The poor have rights. "A righteous person knows the rights of the poor; a wicked person does not understand such knowledge" (29:7 my translation). In another saying God is identified with the poor, making actions toward the poor equivalent to actions toward God. "He who oppresses the poor insults his Maker, but he who is kind to the needy honors him" (14:31).

Though the prudent person is warned not to lend, in the case of the poor the opposite behavior is urged. "The one who is generous to the poor lends to the Lord, who will reward him for those deeds" (19:17 my translation). Again God and the poor are identified so that right relations with the poor is lending to God. This behavior is so fundamental to right order that the king who judges the poor with equity "will have his throne established forever" (29:14).

These astonishing sayings contradict the notion that wealth is equivalent to righteousness. In them the poor are raised to the highest dignity. They and the rich are regarded as equals, but the poor alone are identified with God. God's relationship with them is so complete that actions toward the poor are indistinguishable from actions toward God. No such claim is made for the rich. God's identification with the poor is unique. Consequently, the wealthy and the powerful are warned that to violate or oppress the poor is equivalent to blaspheming against the Creator.

Finally, though Proverbs judges wealth to be a great good in life, it is only a relative good. "Better is a little fear of the Lord than great treasure and trouble with it" (15:16). Or, "better is a dinner of herbs where love is than a fatted ox and hatred with it" (15:17). Conversely, it is better to be poor than to be a fool (19:1), or to be poor than to be a liar (19:22b), or to be poor than to lose your good name (22:1). Wise persons know that poverty is not always the worst tragedy in life. A greater tragedy is to lose one's integrity. "Treasures gained by wickedness do not profit. . . " (10:2; 20:7; 21:6). And though wealth brings safety, it is not wealth which gives one a flourishing future. "The one who trusts in wealth will fall, but the righteous will flourish like the leaves" (11:28 my translation).

3

THE WISDOM WOMAN

In extended metaphors and narrative poems, chapters 1-9 of Proverbs sum up the more diffuse wisdom teachings of the proverbial collection in cc 10-31. Cc 1-9 were added to the older collections of proverbs much later, sometime after the Exile in the sixth century, B. C., and they act as a theological introduction to the old sayings. In this chapter the central metaphor of cc 1-9, the Wisdom Woman is discussed, and this poetic female figure is followed to other texts which speak of her, Proverbs 31:10-31; The Song of Songs; Sirach 24 and Wisdom 7-9.

The Wisdom Woman

At the center of the Wisdom Literature stands a beautiful and alluring woman. She is Lady Wisdom or, as I prefer to call her, the Wisdom Woman. The primary mode of being of the Wisdom Woman is relational. In all the texts where she appears, the most important aspect of her existence is her relationships. Her connections extend to every part of reality. She is closely joined to the created world; she is an intimate friend of God; she delights in the company of human beings. No aspect of reality is closed off from her. She exists in it as if it were a tapestry of connected threads, patterned into an intricate whole of which she is the center.

To follow the Wisdom Woman, to become wise, is to awaken to, and to participate in, this matrix of relationships. It is to take a communal, holistic stance toward the world and its inhabitants, to live in communion with all that is. It is to leave behind the illusion of isolation, that we each live alone, that our personal safety is all. To follow the Wisdom Women is to make a choice for life in its most complete and wholesome possibility.

The Choice

In the collected sayings of Proverbs (cc 10-29), the decision to become wise is presented as a continuing series of practical choices made throughout life. In contrast, in the first nine chapters of Proverbs and in other passages sprinkled throughout the wisdom corpus, this choice is portrayed as the single major decision of a lifetime. It is the choice of a young man deliberating between two women, one of whom he must choose for a life's companion. One is the seductress, Lady Folly or the "Strange Women," whose friendship leads to death; the other is the Wisdom Woman, whose intimacies bring blessing, life and relationship overflowing with peace and joy. Each woman symbolizes a stance toward life and the world and the inexorable consequences of taking that stance. The images of the young man choosing a marriage partner underscore, in the most concrete terms, the seriousness of choices involved in gaining wisdom.

The personification of wisdom and folly in female figures appears, at first glance, to offer women a niche of their own in the biblical traditions, which are overwhelmingly masculine in language, imagery and experience. But that is not the case. This is no safe haven for women, at least not without first making some critical distinctions.

Both women, the WisdomWoman and the Strange Woman, are male projections of opposing aspects of the human condition onto female figures. That is, these are not women as they were in Israelite society or in other societies in the ancient world, nor are they women as we exist today. They are stereotypes of womanhood as men envisioned it. The Wisdom Woman and the Strange Woman are dialectical opposites. One is everything good: valuable, humanly desirable, beautiful and profitable for men. The other is everything harmful to men: the path to death, the speaker of lying words, the source of stolen pleasures. No woman, no human being, is all that good or all that bad. Both women are alluring; both attract helpless men who can barely resist their power, who require every effort of the intellect and will to avoid being duped by the wrong woman.

The Wisdom Woman and the Strange Woman are idealized

images created by men. As literary and religious figures who still live, albeit marginally, in the Church, in general literature and in the imaginations of the believing community, they are harmful to women. In the first place, they are images of womanhood invented by men and not by women whose reality they claim to embody. However, the real harm done to women lies in the stereotypical and dualistic nature of the figures. The images of the Wisdom Woman and of the Strange Woman perpetuate the inhuman stereotypes of women as the madonna or the whore, the object of man's choice to lead him to life or to death. In such a view of the sexes, women are the cause of good and of evil and men are their beneficiaries or their victims. In real life, of course, this is not true. Both women and men are good and evil; both are responsible for their own choices, and neither sex in itself can be totally blamed or totally excused.

Furthermore, many of the depictions of women in the wisdom literature besides the Wisdom Woman are thoroughly misogynist. For instance, "Like a gold ring in a swine's snout is a beautiful woman without discretion" (Prov 11:22). Or, "It is better to live in a corner of a housetop than in a house shared with a contentious woman" (Prov 21:9). And then there is Sirach's view of womankind: "From a woman sin had its beginning, and because of her we all die" (Sir 25:24).

Because it reinforces gender stereotypes about both women and men, the wisdom literature must be approached with critical caution. This means that we must be conscious of its prejudices against women and of its exclusion of women's experience from its purview. Otherwise its powerful word will only continue to harden gender prejudices which dwarf humanity and which negate the lives of women.

If these stereotypical and harmful images of women conveyed the entire story of the women in the wisdom literature, I would not be writing this book. However, there is much more to be found there. The figure of the Wisdom Woman ultimately transcends narrow female stereotypes to take on, in the texts and in our imaginations, a life of her own. More than a typical potential marriage partner, she becomes a developed character in her own right, *hokmah, sophia,* inviting everyone ito full human existence. She is the bridge between God and humans and between humans and the created world. And though for some it is controversial to make this assertion, it seems quite clear to me that in some of the texts the Wisdom Woman comes to represent God herself.

On the other hand, the Strange Woman (see Prov 2:16-19; 5:1-6; 7:6-27; 9:13-18), the wicked woman who represents folly and deadly error, falls away in importance, never to be developed as a character. She herself dies the death in the literature, if not in our imaginations, that she symbolizes in the text. As the Wisdom Woman takes on life far beyond the stereotypical feminine ideal, the Strange Woman disappears altogether. Moreover, as the Wisdom Woman grows in importance, beauty and divinity, feminine stereotypes are potentially broken for us all.

In this vein, it is so rare in the biblical traditions to come upon a female being of importance that an encounter with the Wisdom Woman evokes astonishment. Until recently, scholarly preconceptions have tended to underplay her significance in the religious life of Israel and Christianity. However, I am convinced that she brings with her a vision of reality filled with hope and promise for our fragmented, peaceless world. A recovery of the traditions about her not only offers us female religious symbols much needed today, but also provides material to help us imagine and to create a better world.

A *Figure of Poetry*

Who is the Wisdom Woman? Where can we find her? Will she find us? The answers to these questions are veiled in poetry. She is, preeminently, a poetic figure who appears in some important wisdom passages: Prov 1:20-33; 3:13-18; 4:5-9; 8:1–9:5; 31:11-31; Sir 24; 51; Wis 7-9 and, I believe, in the Song of Songs. (Job 28 and Bar 3- 4 also personify wisdom, but I do not treat these texts here.) It is clear from this listing that the poems about her are not gathered in one place in some systematic way but are scattered throughout the wisdom corpus. That the Wisdom Woman is a figure of poetry means that she can and should be understood on many intertwined levels of meaning rather than in a linear, flat way. As a poetic character she represents an insight into the nature of reality in a way designed to evoke emotional and intellectual responses from the readers. Poetry creates imaginative worlds of beauty to do precisely that. Its truth is determined by the degree to which its imaginative world accurately represents reality. As a poetic figure, therefore, the Wisdom Woman articulates an intuition about reality, and she evokes an intellectual and emotional response from the reader.

This means that the Wisdom Woman cannot be reduced to a list of functions which she performs in the cosmos, though that can be given. She is much more than what she does. She brings with her an aura, a haunting series of hints, allusions and revelations about the world and about God. In the riddle she poses for us to unravel, she is a metaphor leading us into deepest mystery. In her, the term *hokmah* moves from a simple category to describe behavior and qualities of human beings to include a person who is herself Wisdom. The Wisdom Woman does not simply act in wise ways, nor is she a person who is said merely to be wise through and through, though she is that. She is Wisdom. She incarnates Wisdom in all its aspects.

Her Origins

That the Wisdom Woman is no ordinary human is clear from the traditions about her beginnings, or, more precisely, her origins before the beginning of anything else. In an extraordinary poem in Proverbs 8, the Wisdom Woman tells the story of her own birth.

> The Lord created me at the beginning of his work,
> the first of his acts of old.
> Ages ago I was set up,
> At the first, before the beginning of the earth.
> When there were no depths I was brought forth,
> when there were no springs abounding with water.
> Before the mountains had been shaped,
> before the hills, I was brought forth;
> before he had made the earth with its field,
> or the first of the dust of the world.
> When he established the heavens, I was there,
> when he drew a circle on the face of the deep,
> when he made firm the skies above,
> when he established the fountains of the deep,
> when he assigned to the sea its limit,
> so that the waters might not transgress his command,
> when he marked out the foundations of the earth,
> then I was beside him, like his master workman;
> and I was daily his delight,
> rejoicing before him always,
> rejoicing in his inhabited world
> and delighting in the children of humans (8:22-31).

Speaking in the first person, the Wisdom Woman goes on from her beginnings to describe the wondrous events of God's creation of the universe which her creation preceded.[1] Before the formation of the natural realities which human beings take utterly for granted, things which seem to have existed forever, she was created. Before springs and mountains and hills, before dust and seas and the skies above, before the shaping of the sanctuary of the world which human beings were to inhabit— before all these, she was born. The Hebrew word *'olam* translated above as "ages ago" (8:22), literally means "from eternity" or "from everlasting," that is, from beyond measurable time. In poetic language that takes us across the doorstep of imponderables, the Wisdom Woman claims to have existed forever.

It is these origins before the birth of the world which establish the Wisdom Woman's authority. In the ancient world, the older the religious figures and traditions were believed to be, the more claim they had to reveal hidden truths. She is older than even the oldest thing we know, the earth itself. By placing her birth before creation, the author gives her unquestionable authority to speak the truth. This Wisdom Woman is an ancient power to be reckoned with.

However, the poem does not speak of her precedence before creation merely to assert her authority. It makes her an ancient figure also to describe her relationship with the world. Coming before it, she was both a witness to, and a participant in, God's creative activity. She was there when it all happened. "When he established the heavens, I was there" (8:27). "When he marked out the foundations of the earth, I was beside him" (8:30). She saw it all and she can testify to it, but she was not a

---

[1]Bruce Vawter, "Prov 8:22: Wisdom and Creation" in *The Path of Wisdom: Biblical Investigations,* (Background Books 3; Wilmington: Michael Glazier, 1986) 161-177; and further philological discussion in Vawter's "Yahweh: Lord of the Heavens and the Earth," *Catholic Biblical Quarterly* (1986) 461-467.

passive spectator of God's work.[2] She participated in it as his chief artisan. If the text can be trusted, the poem portrays the Wisdom Woman as the chief executor of the architectural plans of the Creator.[3] As chief architect, the Creator determines, shapes, limits boundaries, creates the blue prints which the Wisdom Woman executes. She is the skilled craftswoman, the artist who forms, molds and colors the world. The mysterious beauty and orderliness of the created world sprang from the touch of this woman.

In this poem the Wisdom Woman does not act alone. She is not God, but God's companion. "When he established the heavens, I was there. . . . When he marked out the foundations of the earth, then I was beside him," his companion, his co-worker, "and daily his delight, rejoicing before him always" (8:30). This poem depicts a puzzling mutuality in her relationship with God. She is ever with him, joining in his work, imprinting it with her artistry, and living with God in mutual delight.

What should we make of this poetic vision of the Wisdom Woman's intimacy with the divine? What revelations are contained in the poetic intimations of two lovers joined in a world transcending the universe, yet one with it? For Israel's God is one, and that God has no consort; that God transcends sexuality. Such is Israel's insistence in the face of the manip-

[2]Roland E. Murphy ("Wisdom Theses and Hypotheses," in *Israelite Wisdom: Theological and Literary Essays in honor of Samuel Terrien, ed.* John G. Gammie, et al.; New York: Union Theological Seminary, 1978, 39) also observes that Wisdom's relation to creation is not that of a "casual bystander."

[3]The Hebrew word *'amon* could also be read "nursling," "darling," "confidante." R.N. Whybray reports on the linguistic difficulties of this word and others in the poem in *Wisdom in Proverbs: The Concept of Wisdom in Proverbs 1-9,* (Studies in Biblical Theology; Naperville: Alec R. Allenson, 1965) 98-103.

ulative, sexual conceptions of the divine in the nations around it. Perhaps, it is merely to show the importance of Wisdom that this poem stresses the Wisdom Woman's connection with God. Perhaps, it is to dramatize God's relationship with the world that the poem speaks of her relationship to the act of creation. Or, perhaps, there is more implied here. To ascertain that, though, it is necessary to examine her portrait in other texts. Let it be said simply that, whoever she is, the Wisdom Woman's preeminent status is assured and her company is of the highest sort.

The poem in Proverbs 8 has not yet reached its goal. It has not yet driven to its main point, the completion of the roles of the Wisdom Woman. Her birth before the creation of the world, her intimate part in creation and her relationship of love with its Creator are prelude to her current preoccupation—rejoicing in the inhabited world and delighting in the children of humans (8:31). It is to this announcement that the poem presses. Human beings and the world they inhabit are her interests. By making this her primary role, the poem asserts the immense dignity of human beings upon whom this mysterious figure sets her loving gaze.

The three-fold cause of her rejoicing, God, the world and its human occupants, make her the center of a matrix of relationships.[4] In this poetic vision, it is she who communicates among them; it is she who acts as the bridge between God, humans and the world. She reveals the world and God in their mystery and wonder to human beings. Through her, human beings gain access to God and to the secrets of the world. She is the

---

[4]See Gale Yee's somewhat technical rhetorical study of this poem "An Analysis of Prov 8:22-31 According to Style and Structure," *Zeitschrift für die alttestamentliche Wissenschaft* 94 (1982) 58-66.

key to human enlightenment. By following her, by uniting with her, wide vistas open to humans. Through her the world becomes intelligible and God can be known. From her comes understanding of reality and of humanity's place within it.[5] This is no purely intellectual heritage that she bequeaths to humans, but an enlightenment which fills the whole person, giving peace to the soul and conferring blessing on all of one's existence.

Her Relationship to Human Beings

The Wisdom Woman's relationship to human beings is the central point of these lyrical texts. Though many verses speak of her glorious attributes, her powers and her beauty, these, too, serve to show how valuable she is for human beings to know and to love. As in all true relationships, human alliances with the Wisdom Woman are reciprocal. She takes the initiative; humans respond with every possible effort.

Her Initiative

The Wisdom Woman appears suddenly in the market place, with no warning, with no history of her life beyond that of her supra-terrestrial origins. It is the suddenness of her appearances that make them resemble epiphanies. Her appearances (Prov 1:20-32 and 8:1-19) are reminiscent of a scene in the film, "Raiders of the Lost Ark." The setting is a kasbah or Arabian market place, filled with white-robed people going about their trades. Suddenly, the crowd separates and right

[5]Hans-Jurgen Hermisson, "Observations on the Creation Theology in Wisdom," in *Creation in the Old Testament*, ed. Bernhard W. Anderson, (Issues in Religion and Theology 6; Philadelphia: Fortress, 1984) 118-134.

before us is the startling figure of a black robed, sword-wielding adventurer. It is the shocking suddenness of the figure's appearance, the sense of mystery evoked as the crowd clears, and the immediacy of the figure's gaze as he peers out at the audience, that evokes the wisdom texts.

The Wisdom Woman appears abruptly in the streets of the market place, on the top of the city walls, at the entrance of the city gates (1:20). These are all places where crowds gather, where people come together to transact daily commerce and legal dealings in the ancient cities. In the thick of life at its shabbiest and its most exciting, in the routine of daily marketing and in the struggles of ordinary people to survive—it is there that the Wisdom Woman extends her invitation.

The Urgency of her Invitation

The poem in Proverbs 1:20-33 opens with four parallel phrases.

> In the street Wisdom shouts with joy;
> in the markets she lifts up her voice;
> on the top of the walls she calls;
> at the entrance of the city gates she speaks her words (1:20-21)
> [My translation].

The first phrase of each clause identifies the places where the Wisdom Woman's invitation is issued—in the streets, in the market square, in the bustling opening of the city gates, in the midst of urban life. She delivers her invitation in four ways: she shouts with joy, she lifts up her voice, she calls, she speaks her words. She extends her invitation by her voice, by her spoken word, trying to catch the attention of everyone in the town.

In this poem and also in 8:1-3, the Wisdom Woman appears in the guise of an Old Testament prophet—one who goes about public places, inviting the people to listen to her words for the sake of their lives. In 1:22-33, she implores all within earshot, everyone who can hear her, to turn to her words, to accept her advice, because it is a matter of life and death. The audience are the simple, the foolish, the scorners (1:22; 8:5)—all who have not acquired wisdom. It is these, that is, everyone, whom she begs to accept her promises.

Her Promises

To the one who will listen, her promises are startling.

> Give heed to my reproof;
> Behold, I will pour out my thoughts to you;
> I will make my words known to you (Prov 1:23)

According to the RSV translation, what the Wisdom Woman promises is to reveal her thinking to her listeners. However, another translation is possible.

> Look, I will pour out my spirit upon you,
> I will make my words known to you.

Though the Hebrew word which I have translated "spirit," *ruah*, can mean "mind," or in the case of the RSV version, "thoughts," "spirit" or "breath" are its more common translations. If the second clause of v. 23 is parallel with the third clause; that is, if "I will pour out my spirit (*ruahi*)" is synonymous with "I will make my words known to you," then *ruahi* is best translated "my thoughts" following the RSV. That is, the Wisdom Woman offers her words to those who accept her. However, another kind of parallelism exists in

Hebrew in which one clause extends or makes more specific the preceding general statement. If this is the kind of parallelism used here, the verse should be translated literally, "I will pour out my spirit upon you." The Wisdom Woman would then be saying that she would give herself to the listener, and one facet of that gift would be "making known her words."

At the least, in this verse the Wisdom Woman promises to reveal her message, her words, her wisdom to the ones who accept her invitation. However, far more seems to be implied here. The Wisdom Woman promises her followers to give herself completely, fully, personally to them, to enter into relationship with them in which she reveals all that she is. This is a promise that is reserved for God alone in the scriptures.[6]

However, as Roland Murphy argues, this gift of herself is neither comforting nor encouraging.[7] Instead, it is a sharp rebuke in the tradition of prophetic speech in which God's revelation to the people condemns them because they rejected words of life. The purpose of the poem in Proverbs is to emphasize the life and death stakes involved in human relationship with the Wisdom Woman. This poem draws an analogy between relationship with her and relationship with God. To refuse either is to condemn oneself to death.

The more appealing poem of 8:1-21 also invites the foolish and simple to hear her words of surpassing value (vv 5-9). Here she claims that her instruction, her message, is of more

[6]This point is also made by Terence Forestell, "Proverbs," *Jerome Biblical Commentary*, ed., R.E. Brown, et al., (Englewood Cliffs: Prentice Hall, 1968) 497.

[7]"Wisdom's Song: Proverbs 1:20-33," *Catholic Biblical Quarterly* 48/3 (1986) 456-460.

value to people than silver, gold or anything else people might desire (vv 10-11). But the poem withholds a precise description of what she offers. Instead, it tells us about her.

> I, wisdom, dwell in prudence, and I find knowledge and discretion.
> The fear of the Lord is hatred of evil.
> Pride and arrogance and the way of evil and perverted speech I hate.
> I have counsel and sound wisdom, I have insight, I have strength.
> By me kings reign, and rulers decree what is just;
> by me princes rule, and nobles govern the earth.
> I love those who love me, and those who seek me diligently find me.
> Riches and honor are with me, enduring wealth and prosperity.
> My fruit is better than gold, even fine gold, and my yield than choice silver.
> I walk in the way of righteousness, in the paths of justice,
> endowing with wealth those who love me, and filling their treasuries (8:12-21).

The claims of this woman are extraordinary. "She dwells in prudence"; she "finds knowledge and discretion" (8:12); she has "counsel, sound wisdom, insight and strength" (8:16); and she "loves those who love her" (8:17a) and endows them with treasures (8:21b). It is she who is the content of her message. She loves her followers and in relationship with her, they find life. Here we are close to the point made in 1:23. She gives herself, but in this instance, her self-gift is accompanied with overflowing gifts for human happiness, riches, honor, enduring wealth and prosperity.

An Inclusive Invitation

The Wisdom Woman invites everyone in the midst of life to choose her. In a narrative poem in Proverbs 9:1-5, she builds a house for herself.[8] She slaughters beasts, mixes wine and prepares the table for a festive banquet. Then she sends out her maids "to call from the highest places in the town," to invite all the people to come to the feast. It is a feast for the "simple," those still without wisdom, and the feast will give them life. To come to her table is to live in community, to share in the rich abundance of human life. From this table no one is excluded; at this table no one's welfare is sacrificed for the sake of the few. The festive banquet is an image of human life in which all peoples, from the least to the greatest, live in communion with one another and partake together in the abundant material blessings of the universe. At the feast, the Wisdom Woman presides.

Human Effort

However, to eat at her festive banquet one thing is required. The disciples must choose to accept the invitation. They must decide to put aside simpleness, wrong choices, and the way of folly, isolation and death. They must decide to live in community as full human beings. Because human involvement is essential to this relationship, people cannot be passive beneficiaries of the Wisdom Woman's profligate giving. Personal choice will determine who will eat at the table. Not everyone

[8]The seven pillars of the house have been much debated. For example, see R.N. Whybray, *The Book of Proverbs* (Cambridge Bible Commentary; Cambridge: University Press, 1972) 54; and Dermot Cox, *Proverbs. Ecclesiastes* (Old Testament Message 17; Wilmington: Michael Glazier, 1982) 160.

attends the feast, because many refuse her invitation and reject relationship with the Wisdom Woman.

> Because they hated knowledge and did not choose the fear of the Lord,
> would have none of my counsel, and despised all my reproof,
> therefore they shall eat the fruit of their way and be sated with their own devices.
> For the simple are killed by their turning away and the complacence of fools destroys them;
> but the one who listens will dwell secure and will be at ease, without dread of evil (Prov 1:24-33).

As in every relationship, life with the Wisdom Woman requires attentiveness and sustained human effort. Her affections are not given lightly. The disciple must pursue her with every energy, with single-minded effort, as one pursues a lover. Those who wish to gain wisdom must be seekers. They must look for her, find her, acquire her, gain her (3:13). They must "lay hold of her" and "hold her fast" (3:18). And they must be persistent and vigilant, "watching daily" at her gates, waiting at her doors (8:4). Wisdom is hidden and must be hunted out and patiently discovered. Her followers are people who seek truth, who have not got life's questions definitively settled. They are expectant people for whom life is ever revelatory.

In the poetry of Proverbs, these tensive human efforts involve a decisive seeking with rewards beyond the most exuberant dreams (3:15). The Wisdom Woman's incomparable value is exalted to encourage the listeners to persist in their search. She is beyond comparison with gold, silver, jewels, riches. Her true value is her connection with life. She carries life in her right hand (3:16), and she is a "tree of life," the staunch bearer and sustainer of life to all who hold her in their decisive grasp (3:18).

Throughout the poems about her, the descriptions of her value remain impressionistic in style and content. She is worth more than money and jewels; yet she dispenses them to her followers. She gives life, is a tree of life, yet the nature of this life remains obscure. Is this simply physical life which she grants, or is it a fabric of life, richly textured, fully human and filled with pleasantness and peace (3:17)? The ambiguities and vague allusions are deliberate devices of the poetry. These unanswered questions about the poems invite the reader to puzzle over them, to struggle with them in order to see their cross-fertilization of one another, to find more depth with each reading.

Life with the Wisdom Woman

In the poems so far considered, the Wisdom Woman's origins before the creation of the world and her intimate associations with Yahweh are subordinate to her relationship with humans. This is the principal theme of the poems about her. When the poems describe her, her relationship to the world and to God, it is always to emphasize her value and her desirability to humans and to encourage them in their search for her and in fidelity to her.

To achieve this goal, the sexual imagery of the poems becomes even more explicit.

> Get wisdom, get insight.
> Do not forsake her and she will keep you;
> Love her and she will guard you.
> The beginning of wisdom is this: get wisdom.
> Prize her highly and she will exalt you: she will honor you if you exalt her (4:5b-8).

In the language of love the disciple is urged to live passionately with wisdom as singlemindedly as a lover with the beloved.

The Strong Woman

This thrust of the poems towards intimate relationship with the Wisdom Woman comes to a climax in Proverbs 31:10-31, often called the "Poem of the Good Wife." Many understand this popular piece to be about the ideal wife whom the wise young man should choose to enhance his future. However, recent scholarship takes a different view of the passage.

Rather than supplying the image of the correct marriage partner, this acrostic or alphabetic poem serves as a summary of the whole Book of Proverbs.[9] Its central character is no typical woman but the Wisdom Woman herself. Drawing from images of the young man choosing between the Wisdom Woman or the Strange Woman found in Proverbs 1-9, this poem demonstrates what life is like once one has chosen to live with the Wisdom Woman.

The tip-off to the deeper significance of the poem is the role of the woman in it. No woman of ancient Israel held such a high place in family, society or economy as the poem imagines. No woman held such authority or was granted such responsibility, not even as the ideal. No woman was viewed as the cause of her husband's honor; rather, her husband was the cause of her honor. In ancient Israel, this woman would have been unimaginable as a real woman, and she seems to have

---

[9]Thomas P. McCreesh, "Wisdom as Wife: Proverbs 31:10-31," *Revue Biblique* 92:1 (1985) 25-46.

sprung out of nowhere. However, analysis of the language and content of the poem about her shows that the woman's activities summarize the behavior of the Wisdom Woman toward her disciple.

A rhetorical question opens the poem: "'A strong woman who can find?'" (31:10). Though usually translated "good wife," the Hebrew expression used in this verse to describe the main character means literally a "strong woman" or "strong wife," a "woman of military strength" or "military valor."[10] A negative answer to the question is assumed. No one can find her because she is rare; indeed, she is unique. When the poem discusses her value to her husband, the reasons for her uniqueness become apparent. In themes familiar from cc 1-9, the strong woman is revealed to be no less than the Wisdom Woman herself. "She is more precious than jewels." Her husband trusts her, and he gains abundant riches and honors from his association with her.

There follows a detailed description of the benefits gained from marriage to this strong woman. She looks after every need of her household, from its food to its clothing. Life with her results in constant participation at a grand and festive banquet. To live with her is to become an exalted and noble person, clothed in the purple garments of royalty. The one married to her gains in wealth, security and honor. Because he has chosen her, her husband has dignity and honor among the leaders of the city. She works ceaselessly in his behalf while he gains all through her provident and intelligent care.

The honor and praise lavished upon her by her husband and children do not come from her marriage to him but from the wisdom inherent in her behavior. She possesses many of

---

[10]Ibid., 38.

the traits of the wise person depicted in the collected sayings of Proverbs (Prov 10-29). She labors with discipline and diligence; she cares for the poor; she looks to tomorrow's needs with forethought; she is strong and dignified; and, in the loveliest of phrases, she "laughs at the days to come" (31:25). Her providential care for all in her household, makes of the future a carefree adventure. And central to her identity are her words. When she speaks, it is with wisdom and with the teaching of *hesed,* the word for covenant fidelity and loving kindness.

The benefits of life with the "strong woman," her virtues and her providential care of her family are precisely the gifts the Wisdom Woman promises to all who seek her, love her, and go to live with her. Marry this woman. This is what is urged on the reader of the Book of Proverbs. Live your entire life in her shadow, as her child and her beloved. Become a member of her household. If you do this, you will gain every human fulfillment.

The Wisdom Woman and the Song of Songs

Though few scholars have noticed, the Song of Songs exhibits affinities with the Poem of the Strong Woman in Proverbs 31:10-31. [11]Variously known as "The Song of Songs,"

---

[11]I have found only two interpreters who have identified the woman in the Song with the Wisdom Woman: the sixteenth century Spanish Rabbi, Dom Louis Abravenel, cited in Marvin Pope, *The Song of Songs* (Anchor Bible 7C; Garden City: Doubleday, 1977, 90, 110), and in this century, Gottfried Kuhn, ("Erklärung des Hohen Liedes," *Neue Kirchliche Zeitschrift* 37, 1926, 500-572). However, some early Jewish interpreters associate the Song with various wisdom motifs, including the marriage of Solomon to wisdom. For example, see C.D. Ginsburg, *The Song of Songs* (London: Longman, Brown, Green, Longmans & Roberts, 1857) 22-23; and see Pope, *The Song,* for an extensive survey of the history of interpretation of the Song.

"The Canticle of Canticles" or "The Song of Solomon," this greatest of songs has long puzzled both Jewish and Christian interpreters. Until modern times both communities of interpreters understood the Song as a symbolic account of God's love of Israel or for the Church. However, modern scholarship has made clear that the Song is love poetry pure and simple. As such the poems promote an understanding of sexual love as blessed, holy, a place of divine presence. They provide a basis for a theology in which sexual relationship is whole and redeemed, "a love song set aright."[12]

The Song is a collection of ten or more love poems in which a woman and a man seek love, find it, lose it, and find it again. The poems are strung together in a very loose fashion so that a complete plot cannot be drawn from the narrative poetry. Identification of characters, speakers, even the main threads of the action are difficult to unravel. What emerges is a pastiche of images and moments in the life of love, an impressionistic painting of love appreciated for its own sake.

Common to all the poems of the Song is the central and perplexing role of the woman. She is the main character, the chief speaker, and the initiator of the action. She goes out at night in search of her love. She grasps him and brings him home to her mother's house. She sings his praises, physical and sexual, even as he praises her. She is concerned with her own sexual satisfaction, the disposition of her own body, and she actively pursues her beloved as if women were free to do so in

---

[12]An expression of Phyllis Trible, *God and the Rhetoric of Sexuality* (Overtures to Biblical Theology; Philadelphia: Fortress, 1978) 144-165. For another example of an interpretation of the song as love poetry, see John F. Craghan, *The Song of Songs and the Book of Wisdom* (OT Reading Guide 29; Collegeville: Liturgical Press, 1979).

that society. For a woman of the ancient world, she is completely out of character. In these love poems the actual relationships between men and women in Israelite society are reversed, as they are in the Poem of the Strong Woman in Proverbs 31.

Marriage as a symbol of the intimate connection between the Wisdom Woman and her disciple is the subject of Prov 31:10-31. Life in union with Wisdom is meant to be as close as a love affair or a marriage. Moreover, the language of love appears elsewhere in Proverbs to encourage the disciple to love her, to embrace her, to hold her fast, to live with her (for example, Prov 3:15-18; 4:6-8; 8:17-21).

However, the connection of the Wisdom Woman in Proverbs with the woman in the Song of Songs may extend beyond language to include canonical connections. In the Hebrew arrangement of the biblical books, the Book of Proverbs, which concludes the poem in praise of the strong woman, is followed by two books about women. The first is the Book of Ruth, where Ruth herself is actually identified as "a strong woman"; the second is the Song of Songs. This canonical arrangement is suggestive. Did the rabbis who arranged the biblical books understand both in light of Proverbs 31:10-31? Did they interpret both Ruth and the woman in the Song as manifestations of Wisdom?

In the many layers of meaning that poetry creates, the woman in the Song of Songs is not only a figure of human love, but she also conjures up for the reader, the Wisdom Woman herself. The love trysts of the couple in the Song echo the struggle, pursuit and consummation between the disciple and the Wisdom Woman (for example, compare the following: Song 1:1 and 6:6 with Prov 1:22 and 8:4; Song 3:15 and 5:2-6 with Prov 1:24-31; Song 7:10 and 8:14 with Prov 8:17, Sir

4:12, 18 and Wis 6:12-14). Moreover, like other wisdom books, the Song of Songs is pseudonymously ascribed to Solomon whose marriage is featured in 3:6-11. Later, the Wisdom of Solomon will describe Solomon's marriage to the Widsom Woman (Wis 7-9).[13] Solomon is, of course, the great benefactor and disciple of wisdom.

These connections suggest a poetic coloring for the love poems, an additional layer of meaning in connection with the wisdom traditions. If this interpretation is correct, not only is the sexual arena blessed as good in itself, the Song also serves as a metaphor for Wisdom's relationship with human beings. To live with Wisdom, to pursue her and to be pursued by her, is to enter into a love affair set in a garden of paradise where true human desires will be realized. It is a relationship which itself expresses the harmony and blessedness of the universe.

Her True Identity

Who is this Wisdom Woman, this alluring figure of poetry? Is she merely a literary fiction drawn to contrast a life of wisdom with a life of folly? Is she a personification of the order and harmony in creation?[14] Is she a personification of an attibute of God?[15] Or, is she a divine being, a way of speaking of God in metaphorical language? In the texts about her, there are many indications, connotative rather than denotative,

[13]Sir 51 speaks of Solomon's relationship with the Wisdom Woman in sexual images. See Marvin Pope's discussion, *Song,* 110-111; and the article by Celia Deutsch, "The Sirach Acrostic: Confession and Exhortation," *Zeitschrift für die alttestamentliche Wissenschaft* 94 (1982) 400- 409.

[14]Gerhard von Rad, *Wisdom in Israel* (Nashville: Abingdon, 1972) 145-176.

[15]R.B.Y. Scott, *Proverbs. Ecclesiastes* (Anchor Bible 18; Garden City: Doubleday, 1965) 71-72.

allusive rather than descriptive, that the Wisdom Woman is more than a cipher for the human virtue of wisdom. She is herself God.[16] Much of what is said about her can only be said of God. She existed before the creation of the world and she participated in its formation as a major artisan (8:30). She is a tree of life and in her hand she holds life itself (Prov 3:16, 18). Through her, kings reign, princes rule, and rulers decree what is just (Prov 8:15). She pours out her spirit upon her followers and reveals her words to the ones who seek her (1:23). These are activities of God. They are divine prerogatives, activities to benefit humankind which God alone performs.

In the impressionistic portraits of the Wisdom Woman, there are only hints of her divinity. Never does the Hebrew Scripture suggest that there are two gods, a male and female God, nor does it do anymore than hint that Yahweh has a lover in the Wisdom Woman. In some of the poems about her, the Wisdom Woman remains a creature of Yahweh, though a privileged one, separate from God and delighting in the divine presence. But in other texts the Wisdom Woman represents another way to look at God, another metaphor to speak of the beauty, power and attraction that God holds out to human beings.

In Sirach 24, a poem in praise of Wisdom, written several centuries after Proverbs, the Wisdom Woman's origins are elaborated in a slightly different way than in Prov 8:22. In the Sirach poem she tells of coming forth from the mouth of the Most High; she is the Word of God (Sir 24:3). She is

---

[16]Roland E. Murphy ("Wisdom and Creation" *Journal of Biblical Literature* 104/1, 1985, 9) speaks of her invitation as "the voice of the Lord." Samuel Terrien, *The Illusive Presence: Toward a New Biblical Theology* (RelPer 26; San Francisco: Harper & Row, 1978, 357), refers to her as the "mediatrix of presence."

indistinguishable from God's mind, God's will, God's love. As the Word of God, she "covered the earth like mist," she "dwelt in high places" and her "throne was a pillar of cloud." Like a queen overseeing her domain, she wanders around the universe. "Alone I made the circuit of the vault of heaven and walked in the depths of the abyss. In the waves of the sea, in the whole earth, and in every people and nation I have gotten a possession" (Sir 24:3b-6).

Though imaged differently than in Proverbs 8, the Sirach poem also portrays the Wisdom Woman in the center of a matrix of relationships. She surrounds and explores the whole of the world, the realm of the earth as well as the heavenly sphere, usually reserved for God. She is uniquely related to all the peoples and nations of the earth, as well as to the earth itself. And she is not only related to God, she is God's self-expression. She is God.

Then at God's command, the Word of God takes up special residence among the people of Israel, in the holy tabernacle of Jerusalem (Sir 24:8-12). There the Wisdom Woman flourishes and prospers like trees and vines and gives forth her fruit (Sir 24:13-17). And there she again invites everyone to come and eat and drink of her feast (Sir 19:22). That the Sirach poem is deliberately patterned after the poem in Proverbs 8 is quite clear. And though her roles are the same, she is the thread that ties together all of of reality. In the Sirach poem her identification with God is made explicit.

In a long passage in the Wisdom of Solomon (Wis 6:12—9:18), the last of the wisdom books, claims for her divinity are extended even further. She is described as "radiant and unfading," "easily discerned by those who love her" (6:12) and "the fashioner of all things" (7:22).

"For in her there is a spirit that is intelligent, holy, unique, manifold, subtle, mobile, clear, unpolluted, distinct, invulnerable, loving the good, keen, irresistible, beneficent, humane, steadfast, sure, free from anxiety, all-powerful, overseeing all and penetrating through all spirits that are intelligent and pure and most subtle.

For wisdom is more mobile than any motion;
because of her pureness she pervades and penetrates all things.
For she is a breath of the power of God and a pure emanation of the glory of the Almighty;
therefore nothing defiled gains entrance into her.
For she is a reflection of eternal light,
a spotless mirror of the working of God,
and an image of his goodness (Wis 7:22-25).

To follow Wisdom, to embrace her and to live with her is, finally, to live with God. It is to recognize and to collaborate with the harmony, beauty and order of God in this world and to be transformed by it. This is what it means to become wise.

4

JOB AND THE COLLAPSE
OF RELATIONSHIP

It is very difficult to establish the date of the composition of the Book of Job, but cumulative evidence suggests that it was put into its final form sometime after Israel's Exile to Babylon in the sixth century B.C.[1] However, the poetic body of the Book is framed by an ancient folk tale, perhaps as old as the eighteenth century B.C. If there is neither time nor energy to read the entire forty-two chapters to taste Job's misery, to meet his friends and to decide if his dilemma is resolved, read the following: the Prologue (cc 1-2), the first cycle of Speeches, (cc 3-14); Job's defense (cc 29-31); God's Speeches and the Epilogue (cc 38- 42).

Despite the vision of harmony, order and beauty that the wisdom literature presents, most of the world's people do not experience life that way, at least, not consistently. The Wisdom Literature as a collection is not utopian. If it envisions the possibilities of joy and delight in communion with God, people and the universe, it also recognizes their opposite. The Book of Job is such a story. In it Job's suffering is bitter,

---

[1]For a brief discussion of the problems of dating the Book, see Norman C. Habel, *The Book of Job: A Commentary*, Old Testament Library (Philadelphia: Westminster, 1985) 40- 42.

inexplicable and senseless. Every relationship in his life collapses around him, and his personal world returns to chaos. Ranked among the greatest of the world's literary creations, the story of Job captures the imaginations of believers and unbelievers alike because, in fact or possibility, his story is the story of everyone.

However, it is not simply the content of the Book of Job that works its way into the imagination. It is also the perplexing structure of the Book itself that hooks the reader. Like the pieces of a jigsaw puzzle that have been stepped on and slightly misshapen, the literary components of the Book do not fit together easily. No matter how the interpreter tries to force them, there are always little corners of plot and theme that protrude and leave one wondering. The major structural divisions of the Book are themselves quite straightforward:

Cc 1-2   Prologue
Cc 3-27   Speeches of Job and Three Friends in Three Cycles
C 28   Hymn to Wisdom
Cc 29-31   Summary of Job's Case
Cc 32-37   Speech of Elihu
Cc 38-42   Speeches of God and Job's Replies
C 42   Epilogue

A few examples illustrate the apparently imperfect fit of the literary pieces. For instance, the body of the Book (2:2-42:6) is written in poetry, and the prologue and epilogue are written in prose. This is not remarkable in itself, but the content of the prose does not blend smoothly with the content of the poetry.[2] Another problem is the speeches of Elihu, a fourth friend (cc 32-37), which appear without preparation and add little to the content of the Book.[3] Then there is the major problem of the Speeches of God (cc 38-42) which change the subject of discussion in the preceding chapters from the problem of Job's suffering to issues in the governance of the universe.[4]

Despite the impression of misfitting, however, the parts are generally designed and placed to propel the action of the story forward. They can neither be redesigned nor rearranged without disturbing the artistry of the Book. This indicates that the enigmas created by the structural gaps among the pieces are not haphazard but deliberate. The structure of the Book is itself part of the message. The Book of Job is a sophisticated, carefully crafted masterpiece, designed to entangle the reader in the ambiguities and uncertainties of Job's suffering. The more one thinks about the interrelationships of its parts, the more loose ends emerge and the more possible interpretations appear. This makes it impossible to oversimplify Job's predicament. The wisdom writer employs the *mashal*, the literary comparison or puzzle, to lead us into the enigma of human

[2]See Marvin Pope, *Job*, Anchor Bible 15 (Garden City: Doubleday, 1965) XXI-XXV.

[3]J. Gerald Janzen, *Job*, Interpretation (Atlanta: John Knox, 1985, 217-218), lists reasons for discrediting the Elihu speeches but wisely chooses to keep them anyway.

[4]Robert Gordis, (*The Book of God and Man: A Study of Job*, Chicago: The University of Chicago, 1965, 14-15), provides a survey of the problems involved.

suffering. This chapter retells the story of Job and presents one set of interpretations among many possible ones.

The Prologue (1:1-2:13)

The folk tale prologue sets the scene, introduces the characters, and initiates the action of the Book. It is arranged in five short scenes that alternate between earth and heaven (1:1-5; 6-12; 13-22; 2:1-6; 7-13). The events in heaven determine what happens on earth.

Details of the opening scene (1:1-5) converge to announce the premise of the Book. Job is an innocent man. He is "blameless and upright, one who feared God and turned away from evil" (1:1). The facts of his life provide evidence of his uprightness for, in the world of wisdom, the good are blessed and the wicked punished. A wealthy and honored man, he is respected and loved in his community and surrounded by family and friends. Indeed, Job is so good that he offers sacrifices on behalf of his children just in case they may have sinned inadvertently (1:5).

Should there be any remaining question regarding Job's innocence, God indisputably settles the matter (1:6-12). "Have you considered my servant Job, that there is none like him on the earth, a blameless and upright man, who fears God and turns away from evil?" (1:8). However, it is precisely God's bragging that initiates Job's troubles. A heavenly messenger, called the satan, disputes God's evaluation of Job. His loyalty is not genuine, the satan maintains, but merely the consequence of God's gifts to him. "But put forth thy hand now, and touch all that he has, and he will curse thee to thy face" (1:11). Without explanation God allows the messenger to do with Job as he wishes, "only upon himself do not put forth thy hand."

The satan's only goal is to get Job to curse God.

Back on earth (1:13-22) despite the multiple calamities that strike his children and his property, Job remains steadfast.

> Naked I came forth from my mother's womb, and naked I shall return;
> the Lord gave, and the Lord has taken away;
> blessed be the name of the Lord (1:21).

Unfortunately, this profession of loyalty does not satisfy the satan (2:1-6). The test, he claims, was not sufficiently severe. "All that a man has he will give for his life... Touch his bone and his flesh and he will curse thee to thy face" (2:4-5). Again with God's permission the satan goes forth to afflict Job with "loathsome sores from his head to his foot" (2:7).

Besides the other disasters, Job is abandoned even by his wife (2:7-13), who unwittingly joins the heavenly plot against him. "Do you still hold fast your integrity? Curse God and die" (2:9), she urges. But still Job remains tranquil.

> Shall we receive good from the hand of God,
> and shall we not receive evil? (2:10)

The prologue closes with Job sitting upon an ash heap, surrounded by three friends come to comfort him. So awed are they by Job's pain that they sit with him in silence for seven days and seven nights for "his suffering was very great" (2:13).

First cycle of Speeches Between Job and His Friends (Cc 3-14)

In the poetry the characters change sharply. Patient Job lashes out in anger and despair, and his formerly silent friends harangue him with advice. Nonetheless, the poetry relates directly to the events of the prologue which it attempts to interpret. Arranged in three cycles of speeches (cc 3-14; 15-21; 22-27), the poetry alternates between speeches of Job and his friends. Though the alternation of speakers suggests a dialogue, the speeches actually become spirals of miscommunication and misunderstanding that disintegrate into bitter monologues.

Angry Job

In his first speech Job curses the day of his birth (c 3).[5] Life is so miserable for him that non-existence would have been a preferable fate. Better to have died in the womb than to live to face these horrors. The intensity of his own suffering leads him to ask why anyone suffers, why tormented people are given life at all?

> Why is light given to him that is in misery,
> and life to the bitter of soul? . . .
> Why is light given to a man whose way is hid,
> whom God has hedged in?
> For my sighing comes as my bread,
> and my groanings are poured out like water.
> For the thing I fear comes upon me,
> and what I dread befalls me (3:20-25).

Like food and drink, he partakes of his misery routinely day after day because God has cornered him. This angry lament evokes torrents of anxious words from Job's friends. Growing estrangement replaces their quiet communion with him on the ash heap as their interpretations of Job's life move further and further away from Job's own experience.

---

[5]Job's lament is very similar to Jeremiah's confession (Jer 15:10-21), but no literary dependence between them can be established.

The Comfort of the Three Friends

Shocked at how erroneously Job has interpreted his own life, Eliphaz, the oldest and, hence, the wisest friend, speaks first (cc 4-5). In his view, Job's suffering follows two simple and universal principles: suffering comes from human activity, and it is divine punishment for wicked living.

> Think now, who that was innocent ever perished?
> Or where were the upright cut off?
> As I have seen, those who plow iniquity and sow trouble reap the same.
> By the breath of God they perish
> and by the blast of his anger they are consumed (4:8-9).

However, in Eliphaz's estimate Job may not yet be at the point of perishing. His particular suffering could be divine discipline, "the chastening of the Almighty," a warning for which Job should be grateful because it is temporary. God "wounds but he binds up" (5:17).

Eliphaz reminds Job that once he was a proponent of the same understanding of suffering himself, an instructor and comforter of many. Now, Eliphaz advises, preach to yourself; interpret your own life according to your principles. Were he in Job's shoes, this is what he would do. "As for me I would seek God, and to God would I commit my cause" (5:8). Only in God will he find safety, well-being and a long life ahead because God saves the orphan and rescues the needy (5:15). This advice, he says, is for Job's own good, so listen (5:27).

More acerbic than Eliphaz, Bildad (c 8) begins his recommendations with a theological principle. God is just, he argues, and therefore, God can not be the cause of suffering. "Does God pervert justice? Or does the Almighty pervert the right?"

(8:3) If suffering does originate with God, then it follows that humans are its source. According to Bildad, Job's children died prematurely because they committed sin (8:4). Moreover, it is Job who brought on his own pain and Job who distorts divine justice. "Such are the paths of all who forget God; the hope of the godless man shall perish" (8:13).

However, Job's situation is not completely hopeless. Like Eliphaz, Bildad advises Job to live uprightly and turn to God. If he does so God would surely reward him (8:5). "He will yet fill your mouth with laughter and your lips with shouting" (8:21), for God neither rejects a blameless person nor takes the hand of evildoers. Consequently, escape is possible for Job, but everything depends on him.

Zophar, the third friend, mocks Job and attacks him directly (c 11). From his perspective, Job's complaints are babbling nonsense, "a multitude of words," and Job's torments, even less than he merited. "Know then that God exacts of you less than your guilt deserves" (11:6). Again, the principle of divine justice is at stake, but simultaneously Zophar claims that God's ways are incomprehensible to humans.

> Can you find out the deep things of God?
> Can you find out the limit of the Almighty?
> It is higher than heaven—what can you do?
> Deeper than Sheol—what can you know? (11:7-8).

Because God eludes human comprehension, Job is no less than blasphemous in questioning God. Though Job cannot know the mind of God, ironically Zophar knows. He knows, for example, that God recognizes the worthlessness of certain people (11:11). He also knows that if Job would "set his heart aright" and "put iniquity far away," then security and joy would return and "life will be brighter than the noonday" (11:17).

Job's Interpretation of His Suffering

That the "pastoral counseling" of his friends brings Job no comfort is hardly surprising. His preception of his life contrasts sharply with their understanding. Interspersed with their interpretations of events are his sad and angry monologues (cc 9-10; 12-14; 16-17; 19-21; 23-24; 26-27).

Job's speeches expose spiritual and psychological dimensions of his pain left undeveloped in the prologue. Not the least of his inner sufferings is his sense of betrayal at the hands of his friends. "My brethren are treacherous as a torrent-bed, as freshets that pass away, which are dark with ice and where the snow hides itself" (6:15-16). He tries valiantly to accept their point of view, begging them to show him where he has gone wrong. Then, knowledgeable of his crimes he would, at least, gain peace of mind. However, their explanations of his suffering seem no more than lies to him. "I have understanding as well as you; I am not inferior to you" (12:3). For whatever reason, malice or stupidity, they cannot interpret his experience for him.

But neither can he explain his suffering. Though he knows his friends are falsely clinging to theological principles that do not fit his reality, he cannot produce a satisfactory alternative. The fact of his innocence is his starting point, and that fact conflicts with the evidence of the disasters which have befallen him. These tragedies contradict the theology of which he himself was once a spokesman. Job's suffering, therefore, is compounded by its meaninglessness. There is no higher vision in which to place it and, hence, no way of accepting it and learning from it. Job's world is returned to chaos.

Like Oedipus, Job is driven to find the truth of his circumstances. Since he will not relinquish his belief in his own relative innocence, there is no explanation for his suffering than that God is its source. "The arrows of the Almighty are in me, my spirit drinks their poison; the terrors of God are arrayed against me" (6:4). God causes Job's undoing. "Thou dost hunt me like a lion and again work wonders against me" (10:16). God deliberately miscarries justice.

> Thou dost seek out my iniquity and search for my sin,
> although thou knowest that I am not guilty,
> and there is none to deliver out of thy hand?
> Thy hands fashioned and made me;
> and now thou dost turn about and destroy me (10:6-9).

Since God created him, it seems to Job that God should also protect him and cherish him. Instead, God cruelly sets a trap to destroy him.

Job is not an atheist. He denies neither God's existence nor God's presence in his life. The issue is the nature of that presence which, to Job, seems inimical to everything human. The knowledge that God controls all living things is a cause not of comfort but of terror. If God tears something down, no one can rebuild; if God shuts someone in, none can reopen (12:13). Job's own predicament merely confirms his general estimate of God as the perpetrator of calamities in the world.

But that is not all. God is beyond reach. In addition to intrusive, pernicious involvement in human life, Job accuses God of shunning personal encounter. Against God's capricious dealings, human beings are completely powerless. "If one wished to contend with God, one could not answer him in a

thousand times" (9:3). Like a tyrannical dictator, God deflects
questions and brooks no interference.

> Lo, he passes by me, and I see him not;
> he moves on, but I do not perceive him.
> Behold, he snatches away; who can hinder him?
> Who will say to him, 'What doest thou'? (9:11-12).

Moreover, If Job succeeded in contacting this aloof, inaccessible
being, he would never believe that God was listening to him
(9:16). Communication between them is impossible; Job is
trapped. The very one who should rescue him is the cause of
his troubles and indifferent to his pain.

Yet Job has no recourse but to demand a hearing from his
torturer. Despite the impasse between them, Job's only hope is
to gain a meeting with God. Though implicated in his suffering,
only God can judge Job's case and give meaning to his
torment. Rather than being silenced and intimidated by God's
power, Job grows more and more angry, and out of his anger
Job finds the courage to confront his persecutor, no matter the
cost. "Behold God will slay me; I have no hope; yet I will
defend my ways to his face . . . I have prepared my case and I
know I shall be vindicated" (13:15, 18). Boldly Job makes two
demands of God: that he stop torturing him and that he reveal
Job's transgressions to him (13:21-24). Then Job could go to
his rest.

Job Summarizes His Case

At the end of two more cycles of speeches (cc 15-21 and cc
22-27) Job sums up his case as if he were the defense attorney
in a divorce proceeding (cc 29-31). Nostalgically he recalls
"the days when God watched over me; when his lamp shone

upon my head, and by his light I walked through darkness," "when the friendship of God was upon my tent," and "my steps were washed with milk" (29: 2, 3, 4, 6). In those days, Job's life was filled with harmony and beauty, and his place in the community was assured.

But now "God has cast me into the mire" (30:19). Divine cruelty has replaced friendship. Job's friends mock him, his neighbors abhor him and drive him from the community. Isolated and alone, Job has been violently wronged like a spouse cast aside and left to die in poverty and humiliation.

As if to convince his spouse to come back to him, Job describes his own innocence in a series of sixteen legal oaths (c 31). The traditional statement of an oath in Israel contained an "If" clause, and a consequence or curse. "If I have done this, then let that happen to me"; "that" was usually death. Job states only the first half of his oaths because the incorrect statement of an oath could automatically set the curses in motion.[6] Perhaps Job's oaths attempt to trap God. If they are not true, if Job is not innocent, then God must execute the implied curses. God has to act, but only if Job is guilty. If Job is innocent, God can remain silent, do nothing, but even inaction would be an answer. If nothing happens, then God would vindicate Job indirectly. God does act, not to execute the curse on Job, but to meet him face to face.

God's First Speech (38:1- 40:5)

From the midst of a whirlwind God speaks to Job with a sharp rebuke. "Who is this that darkens counsel by words

---

[6]Matitiahu Tsevat, "The Meaning of the Book of Job" in *Studies in Ancient Israelite Wisdom*, ed. James L. Crenshaw (New York: KTAV, 1976) 341-347.

without knowledge? I will question you and you shall declare to me" (32:2-3). Like the prosecutor in a courtroom, God interrogates Job about his knowledge of the world and his experience of the universe.

> Where were you, Job, when I laid the foundation of the earth?
> Tell me if you have understanding.
> Who determined its measurements—surely you know . . .
> Or who shut in the sea with doors, when it burst forth from the womb?
> Have you commanded the morning or caused the dawn to know its place?
> Have you comprehended the expanse of the earth? Declare if you know all this.
> Can you hunt the prey for the lion?
> Do you know how the mountain goats bring forth?
> Do you give the horse his might? (38:4, 8, 12, 19, 39; 39:1, 19)

Proceeding from inanimate to animate creation, God parades the secrets of the world before Job for his response. Does Job know these things? Does he understand the unfathomable mysteries at the heart of the universe? Of course, he does not, for only Wisdom was present at creation; only she plumbs its depths and understands its secrets. On these matters Job is a know-nothing.

Job's Reply (40:3-5)

Job's reply to God's speech marks another change in his character. Quieted, humbled, Job is more like the patient man of the prologue than the feisty, embittered man of the poetry. Gone is the assured combatant, ready to meet God like a prince.

Behold I am of small account; what shall I answer thee?
I lay my hand on my mouth. I have spoken once,
and I will not answer; twice, but I will proceed no further
(40:4-5).

Compared to the wonders of God's creation, Job is indeed of small account. His troubles are of little importance, they hardly matter, and he silences himself.

God has neither cursed nor condemned him but neither has he addressed Job's misery. Instead, God has changed the subject from Job's suffering to divine governance of the universe. Before God's plan for the world Job can only stand in awe. He seems to have been put in his creaturely place. Because God's authority is reasserted, some interpreters think, therefore, that the poetry should end here and that the second speeches of God and Job are later additions to the Book.[7] Instead, they are the heart of the matter.

God's Second Speech (40:6 – 41:34)

In the second speech from the whirlwind God again challenges Job as if they were equals. This time, however, the subject of the challenge narrows from the universe itself to two creatures within it, the Behemoth (40:15-24) and the Leviathan (41:1-34). In the ancient world these two mythical monsters symbolized the disorder, chaos and wickedness that haunt human life on land and on sea.[8] Symbolically, they

[7]See Pope, *Job*, XXVII-XXVIII.

[8]These two creatures have engendered much discussion. For example, Robert Gordis, *The Book of Job: Commentary, New Translation and Special Studies*, New York: Jewish Theological Seminary, 1978, Special Note 36, 567-568), argues that they are not mythical but the crocodile and the hippopotamus. But see the wonderful analysis of the passage by John G. Gammie, "Behemoth or Leviathan: on the

represent the forces which threaten to destroy the harmony, beauty and order of the world described in God's first speech. The seeming opposite of God's plan, they represent primordial human fears of destruction, disintegration and death, of a world returned to chaos.

God asks Job if he has the power to control these creatures.

> Behold, Behemoth which I made as I made you.
> He is the first of the works of God;
> let him who made him bring near his sword! (40:15, 19)

> Can you draw out Leviathan with a fishhook
> or press down his tongue with a cord?
> Will you play with him as with a bird
> or will you put a leash on him for your maidens? (41:1, 5).

The Behemoth and the Leviathan are fierce, uncontrollable monsters, but for God they are playthings, domesticated and compliant. Because God controls the forces of chaos and death and uses them for hidden purposes, they cannot run rampant over the earth. "Whatever is under the whole heaven is mine" (42:11). Though humans may find in these monsters, terror, evil and death, God has a use for them. They belong in the universe even though Job has no knowledge of their purpose and no power to control them.

Job's Reply (42:1-6)

To these revelations Job responds, "I have uttered what I did not understand" (42:3), acknowledging God's unlimited power and his own lack of wisdom (42:2-6). But it is not

Didactic Significance of Job 40:15; 41:26" in *Israelite Wisdom: Theological and Literary Essays in Honor of Samuel Terrien*, ed. John G. Gammie, et al (New York: Union Theological Seminary, 1978) 217-231.

merely Job's knowledge of the universe that is affected here. His eyes are opened in another respect.

> I had heard of thee by the hearing of the ear,
> but now my eye sees thee;
> therefore, I despise myself and repent in dust and ashes (42:1-6).

He sees God face to face and he relinquishes his claim to be right. Contrary to the expectations of the reader, Job repents.

The Epilogue

In contrast to the ambiguity of the poetry, the epilogue (42:7-17) is clear and crisp. Only God and the narrator speak. God rebukes Job's friends, "for you have not spoken of me what is right as my servant Job has" (42:7). Were it not for Job's prayerful intercession on their behalf, the friends would be lost. Moreover, God announces that Job spoke of him correctly. Then God restores Job to prosperity even greater than before. His brothers and sisters come to him, comfort him and eat a meal with him to celebrate his return to community. His wealth is multiplied, he lives to a ripe old age with many children. His offspring, especially his daughters, are blessed by their inheritance from him. At last Job is vindicated.

The Purpose of the Story

The satisfactory interpretation of this Book requires that its literary components fit together harmoniously. However, the juxtaposition of structural elements of the story raises questions about the story's purposes. For example, why does Job repent? Why does God restore him? Why do God's speeches from the whirlwind ignore Job's suffering? Is the wisdom teaching that God rewards the good and punishes the wicked upheld or overturned? What is the main issue of the Book? The probing of these questions yields implications, possibilities, and likelihoods, not didactic teachings.

Why Humans Suffer

For Job, the most important and agonizing question is why he suffers, and by extension, why innocent people suffer? Several views on the subject, all of which have a certain currency today, appear in the Book. The intense pain and emotion that the subject creates for the characters, as well as the amount of attention given to the question, suggest that it is the main subject of the Book.[9]

Suffering According to the Prologue

The first attempt to explain suffering appears in the prologue. Despite its fictional features, the folk tale prologue gives voice to a very serious interpretation of suffering. It proposes that Job's unbearable pain, and by implication, all innocent suffering, arises from arbitrary divine decisions. Job is no more than a pawn in a friendly game in heaven which completely disregards his vulnerable humanity. According to the Prologue, human beings suffer because they are helpless and unwitting victims of heavenly decisions.

---

[9]My interpretation is influenced by Martin Buber's article, "A God Who Hides His Face" in *The Dimensions of Job*, ed. Nahum N. Glatzer (New York: Schocken Books, 1969) 56-64.

Suffering According to the Friends

Job's friends propose a different interpretation of his suffering. As proponents of the prevailing wisdom theology, they claim that Job's suffering is his own fault. He suffers because he is a sinner, bringing upon himself every disaster. As the guilty one, therefore, he also has the power to end his suffering. It is quite simple; Job must change, repent of his sins and alter his ways. If he does so, he will automatically restore himself to the ranks of the blessed. Humans suffer because they sin.

Suffering According to Job

Job's own experience utterly invalidates the doctrine of divine retribution espoused by his friends. His life contradicts the unbending theory that God rewards the good and punishes the wicked. Job and the reader know that he is not the cause of his suffering; responsibility must lie elsewhere. The Creator of all things must be the cause and source of suffering. This God who once made of Job a friend and bathed his path with milk, now stalks him like a hunter relentlessly pursuing her prey. According to Job, human beings suffer because God, capricious and untrustworthy, turns against them.

God

When the Almighty comes forward to meet Job, one expects to hear a resolution of the problem, but in vain. God's speeches ignore Job's questions. They change the subject from Job's pain to the creation of the cosmos and the animal life that it houses. Consequently, it seems as if Job's concerns are too small to gain the attention of the Creator and Sustainer of the whole world, as if Job's explanation of his predicament were correct, after all.

A few interpreters believe this to be the case. They see in God's reply to Job the imposition of control over humans by a powerful, patriarchal God.[10] According to this view, Job is representative of the human condition in need of further revelation. For them the Book of Job worked its way into Israel's list of sacred books because it depicts the struggles of an individual in need of further revelation. Moreover, they argue, later editors tampered with the Book to make it more "orthodox." This explains why Elihu's speech was included between Job's summary of his innocence and God's speeches from the storm. It also interprets Job's repentance in c 42 as his surrender to a superior, crushing force, and the utter abasement of humankind.

The most authoritative speaker in the Book does not answer the question that appears to be the central concern of the Book—why do the innocent suffer? Though the Book offers three explanations of suffering, none are satisfactory, and the only one who can explain things refrains from doing so. This short-circuiting of the reader's expectations indicates that innocent suffering may not be the principal interest of the Book but only the arena within which to discuss another problem. The real subject of the Book of Job and the crux of the human problem for Israel is not human suffering, but human relationship with God in the midst of suffering. Paralleling the Book's three explanations of human suffering are four ways to characterize divine-human relationship.

[10]See David A. Robertson, *The Old Testament and the Literary Critic* (Philadelphia: Fortress, 1977) 48-50.

Divine-Human Relationship According to the Prologue

In the prologue relationship between God and humans is articulated by the satan. He claims that God and humans relate to one another for purely mercenary reasons. God buys the friendship of Job by giving him gifts; Job is loyal to God only as a consumer of gifts. If gifts are withdrawn, humans will turn away and curse the Giver. Consequently, if the satan is correct, true mutuality between God and humans is impossible. However, the Book itself discredits this interpretation. The satan does not reappear after the prologue because he is proved wrong in the first two chapters. Despite the removal of every blessing, Job remains loyal to God.

Divine-Human Relationship According to the Friends

The view of divine-human relationship promoted by Job's friends is as inadequate as the satan's. According to Eliphaz, Bildad and Zophar, whether or not there can be divine-human exchange hinges entirely upon the moral correctness of human behavior. As in the satan's view, the relationship is still *quid pro quo*, but now the giver, initiator and sustainer of the friendship is the human being, not God. If humans treat God properly, if they live according to the law, righteously refraining from sin, then God will love them and bless them with every good thing. This sort of connection traps both God and humans. On the one hand, human beings must be perfect before God will accept them. On the other hand, God has no choice in the way she treats humans except to execute exacting justice upon them. The friends, therefore, eliminate freedom, mystery and grace from the interaction between God and humans.

Great harm is done to Job by this lopsided theology. Its

pervasiveness in Job's environment magnifies his suffering, and it deafens his friends to the depth of his anguish. Insisting that he is obstinate in his error, they aggravate his pain like sandpaper rubbed against a wound. Intrusive rescuers of others, they inflict their outdated theology upon him and arrogantly try to force him to interpret and shape his life accordingly. In place of God they have put a puppet with strings for humans to pull. Between the Almighty and humans, there is no friendship, only rules to follow.

Divine-Human Relationship According to Job

However, it is precisely the collapse of the friend's theology that plunges Job into an abyss of misery. His pain seems utterly senseless. Unable to interpret it, he can neither accept it nor escape it. Moreover, with the demise of Job's view of the order in the world, he assumes that his relationship with God has also fallen into ruin like a building under the wrecker's ball. Without provocation, God turns against former friends to terrorize and to torture them. God shows no discrimination between the good and the wicked. God is the culprit, the friend-turned-enemy, with vicious intentions toward humanity. Ironically, divine-human friendship is impossible to Job because God is unfaithful.

Divine-Human Relationship According to the Creator

When God comes out of the whirlwind to meet Job, God speaks to Job and Job speaks back. The One who created, ordered and made beautiful the universe and its inhabitants meets Job, appears to Job, addresses Job. Altogether different from Job's description, the Almighty is the Creator, Sustainer, and Protector of life.

The power of the Creator penetrates and shapes the deepest mysteries of the world. He sends the dawn to its post to light the world with pinks and reds, transforming it like sealing wax imprinted with hills and valleys of gold (38:14). The father of the rain and the mother of the ice (38:28-29), she "tilts the waterskins of the heavens" to make it rain upon the dust (38:37). The Creator knows and orders the mysteries of conception and birth and cares for creatures great and small. Even the cry of the young ravens is not too insignificant to gain her attention. Furthermore, the Creator of this exquisite beauty and order also tames and controls the mythic monsters who proudly threaten to return the earth to chaos and to destroy its inhabitants.

The God of the whirlwind is a free God whose range of concerns both includes and trancends human beings. Divine governance of the world exhibits care for, and understanding of, every creature. Human beings are among these. They fit into a world of beauty and harmony; they can see God with their own eyes; they can relate to God in freedom, without constraint. They neither control God nor are they controlled by God. According to God's speeches, divine-human relationship is a relationship of freedom, mutuality and surprising grace.

God of Justice

Though the God of the storm neither explains suffering nor accepts responsibility for it, he does claim to be a God of justice. In the first speech God speaks of the result of divine management: "From the wicked their light is withheld, and their uplifted arm is broken" (38:15). In the second speech

God makes control of evil forces a test of Job's credentials to criticize divine governance of the world.

> "Look on everyone who is proud and bring him low;
> and tread down the wicked where they stand.
> Hide them all in the dust together;
> bind their faces in the world below" (40:12-13).

If Job can do these things, then God will acknowledge Job's supremacy. The Behemoth and the Leviathan may terrify and threaten humans, but for the Creator they are docile, obedient servants. God assures Job that there is justice in the universe, but this justice does not follow the simple equations either Job or his friends have set for it.

Job's Repentance

Throughout the speeches, God's question to Job are rhetorical and imply negative responses. Job does not know how the world was formed, nor how creation occurred and is sustained. The effect of these questions upon Job is to evoke his repentance. The text does not say why Job repents or of what he repents. It could be that Job no longer sees himself as innocent in the face of God's majesty. However, since the reader knows Job is innocent, that seems unlikely. Instead, the text implies that he repents of what he has said about God. "I had heard of thee by the hearing of the ear, but now my eye sees thee; therefore I despise myself and repent in dust and ashes" (42:6). His former knowledge of God had been shallow, empty. God's rebuke was right about him; he spoke "without knowledge" (38:2). Now he has encountered God for himself, he accepts God's view of him, and his whole world is transformed. An experience of theophany, of encounter with God, is the reason Job repents.

The Book explores several approaches to the problem of divine-human relationship and, for important theological reasons, discards all but one. Both the satan and the friends trap God and humans in the relationship. Job sets God free but makes humans victims of God's malevolent freedom. But God releases both of them into freedom and genuine mutuality. Because even in his darkest moments Job never abandoned the possibility of that mutuality, God restores him. Though he accuses God of infidelity, Job's anger at God is a vehicle of his loyalty. He never accepts the ash heap and never allows God to discard him. Moreover, he demands a meeting to set the record straight. When the two finally meet and speak to one another "face to face," the Book's conflicts are resolved; the drama is over. All that remains is the denouement provided by the epilogue.

Job's Transformation and Vindication

In the epilogue, Job's human relationships are also transformed.[11] Because of his intercession on their behalf, God restores Job's friends to divine favor. (42:8-9). Job regains his place in the community and among his brothers and sisters. He receives new children, and his daughters, usually a liability in the ancient world, receive special inheritances.

While a transformation of Job's human relationships is only implied in the epilogue, his vindication is certain. However, rather than extricating the reader from the puzzle of the Book,

[11]This interpretation was suggested in a paper by W. Lee Humphires, "Seeing is Believing: Hearing and Seeing in the Book of Job," Society of Biblical Literature, Annual Meeting, Atlanta, 1986.

the restoration of blessings to Job raises unexpected contradictions. By vindicating the innocent Job, it seems as if the
Book reaffirms the old theology of the wisdom traditions after
all. Has the Book taken us into Job's dark night merely to
reassert the premise that it questioned at the beginning, that
the good are rewarded and the wicked punished? Or has the
account of Job's suffering revealed meanings hidden in the
teaching that God is just?

This Book neither explains suffering nor identifies its causes.
However, it does imply that suffering can be redemptive. For
Job the upheaval of religious faith, of every intellectual and
spiritual certainty, and the collapse of every relationship in his
world lead him to new life. In the view of the ancients, Job was
already dead, without offspring, without community, without
a future. But his place of blood, grief and anger functioned for
him like the earth in the dead of winter. In that dark night he
met his Creator and the whole world was transformed. What
restored Job was not new theology but new experience of the
relationship in which he had participated all along. He gained
knowledge of God in the biblical sense of the term, full,
intimate knowing among loving friends. This is the justice of
God.

The Hero of Wisdom

Job is a hero of wisdom precisely because he obeys wisdom
exhortations at their deepest level. He maintains his integrity;
he would not live falsely with any one, not his wife, not his
friends, not God. Some inner blade of strength enabled him to
insist upon the truth even as he was pressed to settle for lies.
Though his interpretation of God's relationship to humans
was wrong, his perception of the failure of the old theological

world to explain his new reality was correct. He would not deny what he knew. What he learns in the end is that what he knows is only a fraction of what there is to know. Compared to the divine reality, his knowledge and experience are miniscule.

Job as the Struggling Believer

In a prototypical way, Job's experience is the path of adult believers. Often faith begins with inadequate and mechanistic notions of divine-human relationship when we "heard of God by the hearing of the ear." But life impinges. The straight path disintegrates into myriad byways, wrong turns, frightening impasses. In the ambiguity, the horror, even the sin, God awaits, breaking through misconceptions and limitations of divine love so that we can see with our own eyes.

Job as the Struggling Community

However, to limit Job's significance to the prototype of the faithful individual is to read western individualism into the Book. Job's story is the story of the whole suffering people of Israel, a connection little noted in interpretations of the Book. The pattern of Job's suffering and the questions which the Book raises are remarkably similar to those of Israel during and after the Exile. The Babylonian invasion of Jerusalem in the sixth century B.C., caused enormous suffering for the community. Not only did many die in the sieges and their aftermaths, but large numbers of the population were deported to Babylon where they became prisoners of war. They lost their land, their temple, their community life, and many thought they also lost their God.

For centuries the people of Israel believed that God, who

gave them the land of promise, dwelled there with them in the Temple of Jerusalem. Wrenched from the land, from loved ones and from their common life, it also seemed that they had been wrenched from their God who either forgot them or was powerless to defend them. Everything around them returned to chaos and their suffering called out for interpretation. Many of their religious thinkers taught that God rewards the good and punishes the wicked. These included not only wisdom writers such as the authors of Proverbs, but also the Pre-Exilic prophets and deuteronomic writers. Toward the end of the Exile and after, however, the belief that they suffered because they had sinned grew less reasonable. For example, the great prophet of the Exile, Second Isaiah, proclaimed that their suffering far outdistanced their sins (Isa 40:2), and later the prophet Zechariah observes that God was only a little angry but the nations went out of control in applying Israel's punishment (Zech 1:15). Like Job, Israel began to see itself in the role of innocent victim, abandoned by God. Hopeless and without a future, they had lost everything, even their way to understand life.

The author of the Book of Job attempted to make sense of this reality for the community. Why had Israel suffered? There is no unambiguous answer to this question. However, the Book proclaims that God never abandoned them in their suffering, that their suffering had the effect of making them closer to their Creator, a people of dignity, transformed and vindicated. The restored Job is the restored Israel, the tormented and demeaned community reestablished in its homeland, living in harmony and blessing and forgiveness.

Job, therefore, symbolizes not only suffering individuals but primarily the suffering victims of the nations. In Job's story, the hungry, the homeless, the politically and economically oppressed, whole peoples deprived of full human existence can find a mirror of their lives. Job is a symbol of hope that the God who created the whole earth, never abandons his creatures, does not leave the wicked to prosper forever, does not allow the monsters of this world to go unchecked. The Book of Job provides no easy solutions to the problem of suffering, but it holds up for our awe and our puzzlement a people whose God overturns their suffering. Job hints at what will come, the despised and the crucified raised to new life.

The Book of Job, therefore, is a subversive book. It shows God destroying human estimations of the good, the holy and the saved. It declares that God embraces the victims and raises up the foolish according to the world's wisdom. Job depicts the death and resurrection of the people, the revivifying of collapsed relationships and the overthrow of doctrines and ideologies which prevent full human life in communion with God.

5

QOHELETH AND
THE AMBIGUITY OF LIFE

The Book of Ecclesiastes, also known as Qoheleth, is a short
work of 12 chapters. It comprises a collection of wisdom sayings
and reflections about wisdom. The latter are written in both the
first and the third persons and are presented as the final
testimony of a king. The Book was written around the third
century, B.C., at a time when there was growing uncertainty
about the adequacy of the wisdom traditions to address the
problems of believers. Despite its somewhat unstructured contents, the Book is easily read and seems almost modern in its
probing reflections.

The person who meets us in the Book of Qoheleth is one
who has seen it all. He is urbane and sophisticated; life no
longer excites him. Jaded and surfeited by human experience,
he sees nothing new, no possiblity of surprise or wonder.
There is only resignation. Or so it seems.

We do not know this author's name. He claims to be
Solomon (1:1, 12), but that is certainly a fiction. A common
device in the ancient world, pseudonymity gained authority
for a writing by associating it with a venerable ancient person.
In addition to borrowing the name of the wisest King in Israel,
the author also claims a title, "Qoheleth," in Hebrew, and

"Ecclesiastes," in Greek. The title refers to "one who convokes or assembles." Though current translations prefer the liturgical rendering "Preacher" following Luther, Qoheleth probably gathers the people in his role as king rather than as a liturgical leader.[1] Ironically, his use of this title and of Solomon's persona enables him to claim great authority for his opinions, while simultaneously questioning the entire wisdom tradition associated with Solomon and the sages of Israel. By identifying with the King, Qoheleth uses the sages' own ammunition to attack the ramparts of conventional wisdom.

Qoheleth's chief attitude toward the traditions of the past is suspicion. Engaging in what scholars today would call a "hermeneutics of suspicion,"[2] he finds doubtful every conventional interpretation of life offered by the wisdom school. Experience catalyzes his skepticism. What he sees about him and what he observes to be true on the basis of his own experience contradict the teachings of conventional wisdom. For him, honest observation of reality requires the conclusion with which the Book begins. "Vanity of vanities, says the preacher, vanity of vanities! All is vanity" (1:2), a refrain that recurs throughout the Book.

"Vanity of vanities" is the answer to his primary question—what in human life is worth doing? Or as he puts it

---

[1]John J. Collins, *Proverbs/Qoheleth* (Knox Preaching Guides, Atlanta: John Knox, 1980) 71.

[2]This phrase refers to interpretation of scripture or tradition which takes as its starting point the suspicion that particular texts or teachings are biased. Juan Louis Segundo (*The Liberation of Theology*, Maryknoll: Orbis, 1976), describes this theological method as liberation theologians, blacks and feminists employ it. See also Elizabeth Schüssler Fiorenza's (*Bread Not Stone: The Challenge of Feminist Biblical Interpretation* Boston: Beacon, 1984) for a lively application of the hermeneutics of suspicion to the situation of women in relation to the Bible.

variously, "What does a human gain from all the toil at which he toils under the Sun?" (1:3). "What gain has a person from all the toil and strain with which she toils beneath the sun?" (2:22). "What gain has the worker for her toil?" (3:9). To solve this problem, Qoheleth decides to apply his mind "to search out and to seek by wisdom all that is done under the heaven" (1:13). That is, he will investigate every human activity to discern what, if anything, is of value. All the enterprises and attitudes conventional wisdom recommends for wise and good living, fall under his scrutiny.

Common wisdom says it is good to be rich, powerful and famous. It is good to engage in great projects, to accumulate property and wealth and to seek pleasure in every way possible. It is also good to be wise and intelligent. These things make one happy and secure; these things fulfill the human person and gain honor from others, so says society. Qoheleth disagrees. His investigation to "search out by wisdom all that is done under the sun" leads him to startling conclusions at odds with those of his contemporaries.

His procedure is a practical one. The things he wants to learn about, he will do. He will see for himself if these achievements meet the expectations society assigns them. His position as Solomon, King of Jerusalem, enables him to begin his search at the pinnacle of human achievement. He applies himself to learning wisdom, "surpassing all who were over Jerusalem" before him (1:16). He learns wisdom and he learns madness and folly, wisdom's opposites (1:17). He investigates pleasure, cheering his body with wine (2:3). He makes great works, plants vineyards, gardens and parks. He sets up irrigation systems. He buys male and female slaves, gathers wealth and treasure, acquires singers and concubines. Because of all these achievements, he becomes great and denies himself no pleasure (2:3-10). Everything society recommends for human satisfaction he accomplishes.

The results of his investigation are largely, but not entirely, negative. In passing judgment on his labors and on the energy expended to accomplish them, he observes that wisdom is better than folly. "For the wise person has eyes in her head, but the fool walks in darkness" (2:13). That wisdom is superior to foolishness, he knows with clarity. However, in a meaningless world, wisdom offers only a relative advantage. There is no meaning, no lasting significance, to any of the other activities he investigated. "All things are full of weariness: a person cannot utter it" (1:8). "I said of laughter, 'It is mad,' and of pleasure, 'What use is it?' " (2:2). "All is vanity and a striving after the wind," he concludes, and there is "nothing to be gained under the sun" (2:11).

Qoheleth's haunting refrain that "all is vanity" runs through the Book like a polluting stream (1:2; 2:11, 17, 23, 26; 3:19; 4:4, 7, 16; 5:10; 6:2, 4, 7; 8:14; 11:8; 12:8). Though "vanity" is the usual translation of the Hebrew word, *hebel,* its primary meaning is "emptiness," "perishableness." One commentator translates the phrase "vapor of vapors." In Qoheleth's estimate, human efforts amount to vaporous futility, "hot air," that which is empty of meaning.[3] Human reality is void at its center, poisoning all human activity.

The futility of human efforts is not an isolated phenomenon in the cosmos. Like an echo, it repeats the incompleteness of events in nature. Both the human and the cosmic spheres follow an inexorable cycle that is fixed, repetitive, and that never satisfies.

---

[3]Collins, *Proverbs/Qoheleth,* 72.

"The sun rises and the sun goes down,
and hastens to the place where it rises.
The wind blows to the south, and goes around to the north;
round and round goes the wind, and on its circuits the wind
returns.
All streams run to the sea, but the sea is not full;
to the place where the streams flow,
there they flow again (1:3-7).

In the tradition of the sages, Qoheleth maintains that the
natural world teaches lessons for human life. However, his
thinking is distinguished from the sages' by a sharp change in
the content of the instruction. Rather than revealing harmony
and completion in all things, for Qoheleth, cosmic events
monotonously repeat themselves in a closed and senseless
universe. All the laboring by nature's forces amounts to
nothing. The earth is in constant motion, but nothing ever
comes to completion.

Human actions parallel those of the earth. Despite constant
motion and effort, nothing ever satisfies.

"For everything there is a season, and
a time for every matter under heaven:
A time to be born, a time to die;
a time to plant, a time to pluck up
what is planted;
a time to kill, a time to heal;
a time to break down, a time to build up;
a time to weep, and a time to laugh;
a time to mourn, and a time to dance . . .
What gain has the worker for his toil?" (3:1-4, 9)

Using polar opposites to include every activity in between,
Qoheleth affirms the patterned harmony of human activities,
but of what value are they? Human labors repeat themselves

in a fixed scheme, never coming to consummation or fulfillment. There is no satisfaction or closure, only weariness. "What has been will be, and what has been done is what will be done; and there is nothing new under the sun" (1:1). Like Sisyphus of Greek mythology who spends eternity rolling a huge rock up a hill, only to get to the top and have the rock roll back again, so humans are condemned to a frustrating existence. The world drones on and on without hope, with no new possibility.

The Cause of Futility

Qoheleth's inquiries do not remain on the surface of things. They probe beneath questions about the value of human labors to consider the experience of futility itself. Why are human efforts without value? What blocks human fulfillment and satisfaction? What requires the conclusion that "all is vanity and stiving after the wind"? His answer plunges the reader into the deep enigma of human existence. The foundation of all vanity, of all meaninglessness, is death.

Everyone must die. It is death, inevitable and unyielding, that relativizes human effort. This is why wisdom provides only a relative advantage to the wise. The same fate awaits both the wise and the foolish. "Then I said to myself, 'What befalls the fool will befall me also; why then have I been so very wise?', . . . The wise one dies just like the fool" (2:15-16). Nothing that humans do is lasting. Things come and go; people come and go, and not even their memories remain. Moreover, the work a person does, the things collected, the property and wealth accumulated, may at death be bequeathed to a fool. "Sometimes a person who has toiled with wisdom and knowledge and skill must leave all to one who did not toil for it. This is also a vanity and a great evil" (2:21).

Furthermore, death removes any putative distinctions between animals and humans, for both come to the same end.

> "For the fate of the children of humans and the fate of beasts is the same; as one dies so dies the other. They all have the same breath, and the human has no advantage over the beasts; for all is vanity. All go to one place; all are from the dust and all turn to dust again. Who knows whether the spirit of the human goes upward and the spirit of the beast goes down to the earth?" (3:19-21).

It is not only the fact of physical death that disturbs Qoheleth. It is also human ignorance about the fate of the dead. He did not have the benefit of a notion of life after death. That notion is articulated only at the very end of the Old Testament period. To the human eye, animals and humans suffer identical ends, returning to the earth of which both are a part. In the end, therefore, human capabilities provide no advantage over the beasts.

Injustice

Qoheleth's probings uncover still another contradiction of conventional wisdom thinking. The firm tenant of wisdom that the good are rewarded and the wicked punished is not so, says Qoheleth. The truth is the reverse. The good suffer and the wicked "get away with murder."

> "Moreover I saw under the sun that in the place of justice, even there was wickedness, and in the place of righteousness, even there was wickedness. I said in my heart, God will judge the righteous and the wicked, for God has appointed a time for

every matter and for every work. I said in my heart that God is testing the children of humans to show that they are but beasts" (3:16-18).

Trying to reassert the old retributive theology, Qoheleth observes the way things are. Close observation of reality belies the tradition that the good are rewarded and the wicked punished. Following his thought to its logical conclusion, he claims instead that life is wearisome and empty.

A great realist, he is unable to ignore the evil around him. He sees that the world abounds in oppression.

> Again I saw all the oppressions that are practiced under the sun. And behold, the tears of the oppressed, and they had no one to comfort them. On the side of their oppressors there was power, and there was no one to comfort them" (4:1).

To this rigorous thinker the sufferings of the oppressed are inexplicable. The teachings of the sages about the connectedness of everyone in the universe are disproved by clear-sighted observation. The powerful exploit the weak and no one comes to the rescue. The good and the bad both die, and the wicked appear to have got away with it all.

The transitoriness of life causes this discrepancy. Death is the enemy because it cuts off justice. Better off are the dead than those who live under this sentence of oppression. Better still are those who were never born (4:2-3). Life is hateful because in it there is no justice. Human toil is meaningless because its fruits do not last. At the bottom of both is death.

The Human Contradiction

The core of the human predicament is the way God made us, says Qoheleth. Within our very nature there germinates a longing to know the future and to understand reality. Humans yearn to know the beginning and the end of things, but we cannot "find out what God has done" (3:11). Though God has put "eternity[4] into humanity's mind," we can neither grasp it, nor reach it.

Consequently, humans are trapped in a basic contradiction. Straining to understand the eternal, we are caught in a circle of limitation. The future is obscured from us. We can see the present and some of the immediate past, but we cannot reach to the beginning or to the end. Moreover, we can never satisfy our craving to know. "The eye is not satisfied with seeing, nor the ear filled with hearing" (1:8b). Like the unfilled sea, the human person is destined to incompleteness. To be human, in the estimate of Qoheleth, is to be overcome with immense and unrealizable longings. Death, finitude and limitation cut off our hopes and expectations just as the autumn frost sucks the life from the green growth of the earth.

Qoheleth's Negativism

Thus, the Book of Qoheleth approaches despair. Life is futile and human labor empty. To achieve greatness, acquire wealth and wisdom and to become all that society advises is to chase after the wind. We can feel the wind. We know its presence, but we can not see its beginning nor its end. It eludes

---

[4]"Eternity" is the usual translation of the Hebrew word, *olam*, which means "for a long time." James Crenshaw (*A Whirlpool of Torments: Israelite Traditions of God as an Oppressive Presence*, OBT, Philadelphia: Fortress, 1984, 82) proposes reading the word as "darkness." Though this suggestion is interesting, it is unlikely because it flattens out the tension of opposites that Qoheleth sees to be inherent to the human being.

grasp or control and, in the ancient world, it even escaped understanding. The wind sneaks up, touches us and slips away just as life does. Humans understand neither.

Qoheleth's outlook on life is so bleak that, were it not also profoundly honest, it would provoke laughter. To him, nothing deserves human effort because it is all doomed before beginning. Due to his extreme pessimism, many have wondered how his Book came into the Biblical canon at all. But the negativism of Qoheleth, like that of all responsible critics, serves an immensely constructive purpose. His complaints are not futile. He is not a "nattering nabob of negativism," to use a phrase made famous by Spiro Agnew. Qoheleth is exercising suspicion of his society's values.[5] He is attacking the conventional wisdom of his contemporaries at every turn. He is spoofing their point of view and undercutting their shallow philosophy in a humorous and biting way. In doing so, he is acting as the wisest of the wise.[6]

[5]Roland E. Murphy (*Seven Books of Wisdom*, Milwaukee: Bruce, 1960, 103) calls Qoheleth's pessimism a literary device, "an exaggeration directed to attract attention to the 'divine dissatisfaction' that it was his lot to experience in the affairs of this life."

[6]For a more negative interpretation of the Book, see Gerhard von Rad, *Wisdom in Israel* (Nashville: Abingdon, 1972) 226-239; James L. Crenshaw, *Old Testament Wisdom: an Introduction* (Atlanta: John Knox, 1981), and *A Whirlpool of Torment*, 77-92; and R. B. Y. Scott, *Proverbs/Qoheleth* (AB, Garden City: Doubleday, 1965). A positive view of the Book appears in Murphy, *Seven Books*, 87-103; R. N. Whybray, "Qoheleth the Immoralist? (Qoh 7:16-17)" in John G. Gammie, et al., eds., *Israelite Wisdom: Theological and Literary Essays in Honor of Samuel Terrien* (New York: Union Theological Seminary, 1978) 191-204. Dianne Bergant discusses positive and negative views of the Book in *What Are They Saying About Wisdom Literature?* (New York: Paulist, 1984) 57-66.

The Experience of Unknowing

The starting point of his critique is the experience of unknowing as the primal condition of the human person. Humans cannot know the future, fathom life's meaning or understand God's plan.

> "For the human does not know what is to be, for who can tell her how it will be. No one has power to retain the spirit, or authority over the day of death" (8:7-8).

Human ignorance extends from personal matters to the enigmas of the universe. Just as one cannot know the future or prevent her own death, neither can one fathom the deep riddles of reality. "That which is far off and deep, very deep; who can find it out?" (7:24). It is as if a door slams in our faces just as we approach, and in Qoheleth's opinion, that threshold can never be crossed.

In his effort to acquire wisdom for himself, Qoheleth learned that wisdom, as defined by the sages, is unattainable.

> When I applied my mind to know wisdom, and to see the business that is done on earth, how neither day nor night one's eyes see sleep; then I saw all the work of God, that humanity cannot find out the work that is done under the sun. However much humanity may toil in seeking, they will not find it out; even though a wise man claims to know, he cannot find it out (8:16-17).

No matter how much people toil in seeking wisdom, they cannot know wisdom. Many claim to know absolute truth, complete wisdom, but they cannot know it.

It is this theme of unknowing, of the opaqueness of reality, that is the most radical element of Qoheleth's critique of conventional wisdom. In the prevailing view, wisdom is accessible, the divine plan for the world and for human beings is clear and knowable, and God's behavior, predictable. Neither God nor the world is likely to cause surprise, wonder or dismay. In relation to humans, both are transparent.

Not for Qoheleth. At the heart of his suspicions is his own belief that neither the universe nor God is penetrable to human probing. It is true for him that the righteous and the wise are in the hand of God, but whether it is for love or for hate, humans do not know (9:1). God and the divine enterprises are beyond our comprehension, beyond our grasp. God is other and distant. When you pray make your words few, "for God is in heaven and you upon earth" (5:2).

Speaking directly to the proponents of easy wisdom, Qoheleth's first project is to debunk their dangerous half-truths and rigid certainties. With a beautiful image, he offers an alternative stance before life.

> As you do not know how the spirit comes to the bones in the womb of a woman with child, so you do not know the work of God who makes everything (11:5).

The wondrous mystery of human conception and birth parallel the wonder and inscrutability of the work of God. Neither can be understood, then or now. Both realities draw us into vast, whirling spaces where the human mind reaches its limits. Both are described with doctrinaire certitude by narrow minds seeking the security of absolutes.

Though Qoheleth's skepticism might appear to destroy the relationship between God and humans, he accomplishes the reverse. By reasserting the otherness of God, he makes relationship between God and humans possible again. He contradicts the conventional view that reduces God to a human construct. He rejects any thinking that limits, controls and diminishes the inexpressible beyondness of the Living God.

Similar dynamics of restriction occur in human relationships. For example, when the parents of an adult continue to treat her as a child, full communication and love are not possible between them. Or, when one spouse views the other as a fixed personality with no room for change or growth, the marriage falters. In such relationships, individuals, restricted by conceptions others hold of them, are violated and demeaned. They are deprived of the full mystery of their personhood. Qoheleth thinks his contemporaries have violated God in a similar fashion. His writing seeks to free God from human constrictions, thereby enabling divine-human relationships to resume on new grounds.

Knowledge of God

To do this, Qoheleth contradicts himself. On the one hand, he declares God and the divine plan to be unknowable; on the other hand, he claims himself to know a good deal about that God and about the divine plan! For instance, from the hand of God come the gifts of eating, drinking and toil (2:24). God dispenses wisdom, knowledge and joy to the ones who are pleasing to her (2:26). God made everything beautiful and put eternity into human minds (3:11). Whatever God does endures forever (3:14). Therefore, neither human capacity to know something of God nor God's willingness to be known are Qoheleth's main points of contention. The real dispute is what it is that humans can know about God. Obviously, humans can know something of God's activities. But relationship with God requires that divinity be recognized for what it is, undefined, unconstrained freedom and transcendence. The heart of God and the mystery of the divine plan are as inscrutable to humans as the quickening of the fetus is in the womb of its mother. To live in relationship with God, therefore, humans must accept that God is mysterious, free and beyond human definition.

Fear of the Lord

Because God is mystery, Qoheleth urges his reader to "fear the Lord." He uses the phrase or a variation infrequently (7:18; 8:12; 3:14), perhaps to avoid the impression that he is reiterating conventional understanding of it. Though some interpreters claim otherwise, this traditional phrase of wisdom is reasserted in Qoheleth's Book with all its usual force.[7] However, here it is deliberately nuanced by his insistence on God's transcendent mystery. For Qoheleth, the God-fearers are the opposite of the wicked and things will go well with them (8:12-13). In a reflection characteristic of Qoheleth, that promise is repeated.

> In my vain life I have seen everything; there is a righteous person who perishes in his righteousness and there is a wicked person who prolongs his life in his evil doing. Be not righteous over-much, neither be a fool; why should you die before your time? It is good that you should take hold of this and from that withhold not your hands; for the one who fears God shall come forth from them all (7:15-17).

Though one cannot imagine how, in the end, no matter what happens, the one who fears God will prevail. Qoheleth is able

---

[7]Some argue that "fear of Yahweh" conveys the sense of literal fear in Qoheleth, distinguishing its use here from the rest of the Bible. This is denied by both Whybray ("Qoheleth," 201) and Derousseaux (*La Crainte de Dieu*, 337-345). It is my view that such an interpretation has no basis in the text and flattens out the contradictions of Qoheleth too facilely.

to reaffirm the traditional doctrine of fearing God because he balances it with the affirmation of God's mysterious transcendence. For him, fearing God cannot be a way to manipulate and control the divinity.

In chapter 3, where he points out the enigmatic state of humanity's ignorance, Qoheleth brings together the two themes of the "fear of God" and the transcendence of God.

> God has put eternity into humanity's mind, yet so that she cannot find out what God has done from the beginning to the end. . . .
>
> I know that whatever God does endures for ever; nothing can be added to it nor anything taken from it: God has made it so, in order that humans should fear before him (3:11-14).

The reason humans exist in a condition of partial knowing is that they may fear God, so that they may live in awe and in trustful obedience, drawing near to the fascinating mystery of the divine.

To be a creature is not to know, or, in Paul's phrase, it is "to see through a glass darkly." The "fear of God" involves the recognition and the acceptance of this limitation. According to Von Rad's view, there is no knowledge in Israel which does not "throw the one who seeks the knowledge" back upon the question of self-knowledge and self-understanding.[8] In this case, it is the inability to know which provokes this reflection. To be a human creature is not to know. Mortality and unknowing define human existence. To draw near to the Living God, humans must embrace the truth of creaturehood, and in awe and wonder, surrender to the surprising and disturbing love of the Creator.

---

[8]Von Rad, *Wisdom*, 67.

Enjoyment of Life

Despite all his statements to the contrary, therefore, Qoheleth affirms the beauty and the value of human life. One clue to his true purpose is the repetition of the theme that runs counter to the "vanity of vanities" motif. Over and over, he exhorts his readers to enjoy life, to eat and drink and find enjoyment in their toil, for this is what God has given humans to do (2:24; 3:12, 22; 5:18-19; 8:15; 9:7, 9). In his disparagement of human efforts, Qoheleth's purpose has been to show how wrong-headed are the motivations spurring our expenditures of energy. People rarely question the reasons for their mad efforts "to get ahead."

Life is a gift to us. What it is good for humans to do is to be happy in life, to enjoy it, to find pleasure in eating and drinking, and working.

> Go eat your bread with enjoyment, and drink your wine with a merry heart; for God has already approved what you do. Let your garments be always white; let not oil be lacking on your head. Enjoy life with your spouse, all the days of your vain life which God has given you under the sun, because that is your portion in life and in your toil at which you toil under the sun (9:7-9).

From waking to sleeping, the tasks and pleasures of eating, drinking, and working fill the day for most of the world's peoples. Or these activities comprise the simple aspirations of the many who lack them. "Human companionship, genuine society"[9], the duties and small pleasures that make physical

---

[9]A phrase of Joseph Blenkinsopp in *Wisdom and Law in the Old Testament: The Ordering of Life in Israel and Early Judaism* (OBS, Oxford: Oxford Univerity, 1983) 68.

and spiritual survival possible—these are what matter. Constructive work to do, sufficient food and happiness in family life—these are everyone's birthright. And, implies Qoheleth, these are all that is needed. Daily existence with its own rhythms and duties gives life meaning and fulfills true human longings.

> Therefore I commend mirth, because there is nothing good for a person under the sun except eating and drinking and mirth; for this is the accompaniment of his toil during the limited days of the life which God gives him under the sun (8:15).

Roland Murphy's translation of this verse[10] captures the sense of Qoheleth's view. Mirth counterposes vanity. God intends that human beings enjoy life and find delight in their daily activities. Qoheleth advocates neither blind pleasure nor suicidal despair in the face of the abyss. He affirms that life is meaningful when it is lived in simplicity and in the "fear of God." For such people, laughter is possible in the face of death. Such people taste life deeply and live thoroughly in the time granted to them. Though life ends in death, though the unjust appear to prevail, though humans cannot know the secrets of it, life is immensely valuable.

Live Fully

So Qoheleth enjoins his readers to live with energy and zest. Enjoy life in all its aspects. Find pleasure in the simple things: eating, drinking, your daily labors, life with your family. Do not refuse to live out of fear of possible disasters. Take risks. You do not know what fine surprises might come

---

[10]Murphy, *Seven Books,* 103.

your way. "Cast your bread upon the waters, for you will find it after many days" (11:1). All of these things God has given you to do. It is your portion and your lot. And in enjoying your life you please God. You fear God. You obey and love God and live as a truly wise person.

A Mashal

What Qoheleth has created is a *mashal*. Simultaneously, he draws two contradictory pictures of life. In one picture, human existence is bleak, dismal and empty; in the other, life is beautiful, simple and filled with causes for joy and delight. Interpretations of the Book have often stressed its negative vision, while dismissing its positive affirmations. This certainly reduces the contradictions in the Book, but it also completely distorts its meaning. Such interpretations take insufficient account of the use of *mashal* by the wisdom writers. At its root, a *mashal* is a comparison. So is the Book of Qoheleth. It compares the rhetoric of conventional wisdom and his own experience-garnered view of reality. True wisdom and false wisdom are set side by side to create deliberate contradictions. Left intact, the contradictions produce a paradox in which the author only appears to affirm contradictory realities. The purpose of paradox is not to bring thinking to an impasse. Rather, paradox functions to engage the imagination by forcing it to press past the contradictions into the world of mystery.[11] Qoheleth, like Job, leads the reader through conventional thinking and then beyond it to insight about realities that can not be articulated one-dimensionally.

---

[11]James Fischer, "Biblical Paradox" in *Christian Biblical Ethics*, Robert Daly, et al., eds., (New York: Paulist, 1984) 103-107.

A later editor of the Book seems to have grasped the Book's intention perfectly. In an editorial addition, which contains its own *mashal*, the editor provides instructions for interpreting the Book (12:9-13). "The sayings of the wise are like goads, and like nails firmly fixed are the collected sayings which are given by one Shepherd" (12:9-11). "Like goads," Qoheleth's words provoke, prick and prod the readers, stinging them out of comfortable, stagnant lives. Also "like nails," the words of the "one Shepherd" are reliable, firmly fixed, able to hold things in their proper place. His words are truthful. Since "shepherd" is an epithet for the king in Israel, it refers to the author, posing as Solomon. To interpret the Book, readers should understand that it will both goad their thinking and provide reliable guidance. "Beware of anything beyond these" (12:12), advises the later editor.

In his *mashal*, Qoheleth is as wise as Solomon. His suspicions of religious wisdom restore true wisdom. In the manner of the wise judge-king, he cuts through the facade and deceit of the day to discover what the truth really is. He exposes the shallowness and perversion which creep into all religious formulations when they are severed from vibrant relationship with the living God. In accord with the tradition of Solomon, his vision is based on the authority of human experience; it recognizes the unity of human existence with the life and events of the universe; it affirms the centrality of the fear of Yahweh in human relationship with God; and finally, it validates ordinary human life as the arena of spirituality.

Facing the inexorable fact that humans must die, then how shall we live? Knowing that the zest and joy of youth fade daily as we march toward old age (12:1-7), then what is the point of it all? Only to live every minute of it with joy and mirth, to experience life intensely in the good and the bad, not to be defeated by the injustice we see, not to labor for fleeting rewards, but to love and fear God and do fully all God gives us to do. Everything else is "vanity of vanities and striving after the wind."

6

SIRACH AND COMMUNION
WITH GOD

The Book of Sirach, or Ecclesiasticus, as it is also called, was written in Jerusalem around 180 B. C. Jesus ben Sirach's grandson translated it into Greek sometime after 132 B. C., for the Jews living in the Egyptian city of Alexandria. The grandson's prologue introduces the Book, which is an anthology of Sirach's teachings on many subjects. The Book is not part of the Hebrew canon. However, the Roman Catholic and Greek Orthodox Churches, which follow the Greek canon, accept the Book as deutero-canonical. To get a sense of the work, read the grandson's prologue, chapters 1-15, chapter 24 and chapters 44-51.

The Historical Context

The Book of Sirach is a book prepared for a crisis. At stake was the identity of the Jewish community and its belief in the one God. A century and a half before Sirach's time, Alexander the Great (356-323) invaded the entire eastern Mediterranean region including Palestine. With him, he brought his dream of uniting the whole world under the cultural traditions of Hellenism, which at different times throughout the next two centuries, threatened to absorb or to crush Judaism.

Derived from Hellas, the ancient name for Greece, Hellenism refers to the philosophy, religion and culture that dominated the ancient world during the last few centuries before the Christian era.[1] Hellenism claimed to be a superior and civilizing culture. It exalted the human, valued learning and speculated about wisdom and the divine world. When Sirach was writing in the second century, B. C., Alexander's political descendents, known as the Seleucids, occupied Palestine and actively sought to impose Alexander's pan-Hellenic dreams upon the Jews.

To many in the Jewish community, especially the educated, Greek culture and learning were immensely attractive. Some members of the community embraced Hellenism, enthusiastically adopting Greek thinking and customs and even taking Greek names. Others were confused by the conflict of Greek values with their own. Still others fiercely resisted the absorption of Judaism into Hellenism. The results were deep turmoil within the Jewish community, a questioning of Jewish beliefs and practices and wholesale doubt about the appropriateness of their faith for modern life.

Sirach responded to the crisis by writing a guidebook or set of instructions for the young students who attended his school in Jerusalem (51:23). His Book addresses the question, "How shall I be wise?" In response, he articulates a spirituality based on the traditions of Israel and directed toward the problems raised by Israel's confrontation with Hellenism.

So reliant is Sirach upon the ancient teachings of Israel that one scholar calls his Book a "conservative" response to Hellen-

---

[1]For further historical background, see Bernhard W. Anderson, *Understanding the Old Testament*, fourth edition (Englewood Cliffs: Prentice Hall, 1986) 610-618, and Martin Hengel, *Judaism and Hellenism: Studies in Their Encounter in Palestine during the Early Hellenistic Period*, 2 vols. (Philadelphia: Fortress, 1974).

ism.[2] While I think this insight is correct, I prefer to call the Book "traditional." Too often the word conservative suggests a mindless return to former ways of life. Sirach does not resort to the ancient traditions in order to recapture the past. He is a brilliant and inventive theologian who employs old traditions in the most original fashion, reinterpreting them and combining them in new ways. Using the past, he illuminates the present. He unleashes the subversive power hidden in the tradition to challenge the claims that Hellenism makes upon believers.

Sirach neither attacks nor belittles the culture that threatens his people. Instead, he treats Hellenism with great respect, accepting some of its values and taking its questions with utmost seriousness. He absorbs into his vision Hellenism's probings into the meaning of life, its devotion to learning, its speculations about the divine sphere and its desire for wisdom. However, he thrusts aside Hellenism's answers, and he replaces them with answers drawn from the scriptures of Israel. In a splendid *tour de force*, he asserts that only in communion with the God of Israel can one gain Wisdom.

Wisdom

The all-encompassing theme of Sirach's Book is Wisdom or, as she is called in Greek, Sophia. In response to the crisis that Hellenism presented to the Jewish faith, Sirach asserts that wisdom is neither a human achievement, as some Greek philosophies promised, nor is she a goddess of the ancient religions. Rather, Wisdom is the creation and the gift of the God of Israel. This is the main idea of his Book which he

---

[2]Alexander di Lella, "Conservative and Progressive Theology: Sirach and Wisdom," in *Studies in Ancient Israelite Wisdom*, ed., James L. Crenshaw (New York: KTAV, 1976) 401-426.

explores and develops in a variety of themes and metaphors.[3]

Like many of the biblical poets, Sirach's approach is circular rather than linear. His major themes, like fear of Yahweh, Torah and Wisdom, resemble the flames of a fire that lick up around a piece of wood, rising, converging and separating again. Often his ideas blend into each other so thoroughly that one can barely distinguish them from each other. Though this approach can cause difficulty for modern readers, it enables Sirach to examine wisdom from many perspectives and, in this way, to create a new synthesis of wisdom thought.

The Wisdom Woman

Sophia holds up the Book of Sirach the way walls hold up a house. She stands at three key points in the Book's architecture: the beginning (Sir 1), the middle (Sir 24) and the end (Sir 51). From there she structures and supports the Book, just as she structures and supports Sirach's theology. This chapter ap-

[3]Edmund Jacob ("Wisdom and Religion in Sirach," in *Israelite Wisdom: Theological and Literary Essays in Honor of Samuel Terrien,* ed. John G. Gammie, et al; New York: Union Theological Seminary, 1978, 247-260) and Gerhard von Rad (*Wisdom in Israel,* Nashville: Abingdon, 1972, 240-262) also argue that wisdom is the main theme of Sirach. However, James L. Crenshaw (*Old Testament Wisdom: an Introduction,* Atlanta: John Knox, 1981, 149-173) supports those who think fear of Yahweh is the principal theme.

proaches the Book of Sirach through the figure of Sophia, primarily as she appears in the three organizing passages that contain the core of Sirach's message (Sir 1, 24 and 51). Then the chapter turns to some of his practical advice where he applies his theology to the circumstances of daily living.

Wisdom and the God of Israel

Sirach constructs the first wall of his Book with two poems about the Wisdom Woman's relationships (1:1-10 and 1:11-20). The first poem is about her relationship with God and the second about her relationship with humans. In the opening poem (1:1-10), she alternates with God as the subject of the poetry.

> All wisdom comes from the Lord and is with him forever.
> The sand of the sea, the drops of rain,
> and the days of eternity—who can count them?
> The height of heaven, the breadth of the earth,
> the abyss, and wisdom—who can search them out?
> Wisdom was created before all things,
> and prudent understanding from eternity.
> The root of wisdom—to whom has it been revealed?
> Her clever devices—who knows them?
> There is One who is wise, greatly to be feared, sitting upon his throne.
> The Lord himself created wisdom,
> he saw her and apportioned her,
> he poured her out upon all his works.
> She dwells with all flesh according to his gift,
> and he supplied her to those who love him (1:1-10).

The alternation of poetic subjects in this poem creates the impression of a mysterious intertwining of roles and relationships between the two figures. (Sophia is the focus of vv 1-6; God, of vv 8-9; Sophia of v 10a and God again of v 10b). She is as unfathomable as a divine being; God alone knows her and understands her. This is Sirach's point in his opening poem. Sophia's principal characteristic is her distance from humankind. As indecipherable as the riddles of the universe, she is utterly inaccessible to human searching. Her creation before the creation of the world only accentuates her remoteness. Though she is utterly desirable, one cannot gain her easily, if at all, without the aid of the One who created her.

God's role in these verses is to provide humankind with a pathway to Wisdom. While she is distant from humanity, she is intimately related to God. God created her; God alone knows her and is forever united with her. He supplies her to "all who love him." Consequently, if humans wish to acquire Wisdom, they must first befriend her creator. In Sirach's metaphorical language, Sophia is the desirable one, but she can be pursued only through her intermediary who is God. It is he who "pours her out upon all his works," and he who "causes her to dwell with all flesh." For Sirach, therefore, Wisdom has a mission to every people, "all flesh," but God sends her to those who are connected to him.

Sirach's opening poem establishes the bold yet simple claim of his Book: the source of Wisdom is the God of the Jews. However, she is not the sole possession of an isolated or nationalistic community. She has a mission to all people, to everyone who loves God. In language rife with a history of accumulated meanings, Sirach asserts that every human yearning, every inclination of the mind and the spirit, every desire of the heart bound up in the notion of wisdom in Judaism and Hellenism, is realized in communion with this God.

Fear of Yahweh

In Sirach's second poem about her (1:11-20), Sophia is not distant from humankind. Here, identified with the "fear of Yahweh, she is an expression of the human response to God, of the attitudes of love, trust and obedience that humans return to their Creator. Sophia and fear of Yahweh are intertwined as mysteriously and inextricably in this poem as are God and Wisdom in the first poem. Similarly, the subject of the poetry in the second poem alternates between Sophia and the fear of Yahweh, making a separation of the two themes very difficult.

On the one hand, those who fear Yahweh gain Sophia's presence. She is created with the faithful in the womb" (1:14); she lives in union with them, and they trusted her (1:15). Moreover, she satisfies them, blesses them (1:16-17), and she brings them health, peace and long life (1:18, 20). To fear Yahweh, therefore, is to gain Wisdom's gifts. On the other hand, the fear of Yahweh is the full expression of Wisdom. It is "the beginning" (1:14), "the full measure" (1:16), the "crown of wisdom" (1:18), and "the root of wisdom" (1:20). For Sirach, the fear of Yahweh is not simply the way to Wisdom, it is Wisdom.

By equating Sophia and the fear of Yahweh, the sage affirms that she expresses humanity's free response to the transcendent God. Furthermore, in identifying the Wisdom Woman with the fear of Yahweh, he makes explicit what is implied in the poems about her in Proverbs. She mediates in two directions, communicating with God on behalf of humans and communicating with humans on behalf of God. Therefore, from both divine and human perspectives, she not only enables relationship between the two; mysteriously, she is that relationship. Her very identity is the communion between God and humankind; she is the bond of love between them. In metaphorical language, humankind goes through God to reach her and through her to reach God. In answer to the question, "How can I be wise?," Sirach replies, "Fear Yahweh." Thus, Sirach builds the first wall of his poetic house.

Wisdom Torah

The second wall of Sirach's structure, its chief support without which the whole building would collapse, is chapter 24. This chapter is the integrating center of the Book both physically and theologically,[4] and it marks a major expansion of wisdom thinking. In it Sophia is identified with another Old Testament theme, the Law or Torah of Israel. In this chapter the Wisdom Woman herself speaks directly to the audience for the first and only time in the Book, to highlight the importance of the chapter. In all her other appearances, Sirach speaks about her in the third person.

Her Origins

An introductory verse obliquely announces Sophia's speech. She will praise herself in the midst of an unidentified people (24:1). When she begins to speak, however, her location is not among this special people but in the court of heaven. There she proclaims the exalted nature of her origins: "I came forth from the mouth of the Most High" (24:3a). She is born from God, not as a subordinate creature, but as God's Word. She is

---

[4]R. A. F. McKenzie (*Sirach*, Old Testament Message 19, Wilmington: Michael Glazier, 1983, 100) calls c 24 the high point of the Book.

God's self-expression, and God's revelation, and in that capacity she envelops the earth with her presence (24:3b).

Continuing to identify herself with the Creator, she describes her wanderings about the cosmos in language reserved for God elsewhere in the Old Testament.

> I dwelt in the high places
> and my throne was in a pillar of cloud.
> Alone I have made the circuit of the vault of heaven
> and walked in the depths of the abyss (24:4-5).

Though she came forth from God, she can hardly be distinguished from God and from his activities. Moreover, as if all the world were her kingdom and she its queen, she explores the universe and claims every people as her own possession (v 6). However, something is lacking. What she seeks is a permanent abode, a resting place among the peoples of the earth (v 7).

Her Mission

The next verse (24:8) solves the problem of her home by assigning her a permanent residence. Though the whole world is her domain, the Creator chooses a place for her to dwell among the special people foreshadowed in the first verse.

> Then the Creator of all things gave me a commandment,
> and the one who created me assigned a place for my tent,
> And he said "Make your dwelling in Jacob,
> and in Israel receive your inheritance."
> From eternity, in the beginning, he created me,
> and for eternity I shall not cease to exist,
> In the holy tabernacle I ministered before him,
> and so I was established in Zion.

In the beloved city likewise he gave me a resting place,
and in Jerusalem was my dominion.
So I took root in an honored people, in the portion of the Lord,
who is their inheritance (24:8-12).

In various ways, these verses affirm that Wisdom is found uniquely in Israel. It is there that she sets up her tent, there that she takes up residence and receives her inheritance. In the Temple of Jerusalem on Mt. Zion, she rests and she rules. To an age and to a culture which ask where to find wisdom, Sirach replies unequivocally: find her in the worship of the one true God. It is in Israel's worship that Sophia took root and flourished (v 12). There she gives forth blooms, fragrance and choice fruit (vv 13-17). From there, she issues the invitation to her banquet.

Her Invitation

In imagery of love and feasting similar to the imagery of Proverbs 8-9, Sophia invites everyone who desires her to come to her banquet (24:19-23). To those who eat at her table she promises a meal of sweet delicacies and the satisfaction of their deepest hungers. Assumed in these verses is a view of the human condition characterized by profound longing, by an emptiness pervading all human life in its incompleteness. To satisfy those hungers, Sophia claims, one must come to her table and eat of her feast. To this point, the vocabulary of the poem echoes the language of Provs 9:1-5. However, in Sir 24 there is a startling change in the meal to be served at the banquet.

> Come to me, you who desire me,
> and eat your fill of my produce.
> For the remembrance of me is sweeter than honey,
> and my inheritance sweeter than the honeycomb.
> Those who eat me will hunger for more,
> and those who drink me will thirst for more (vv 19-21).

What is to be eaten and to be drunk at the festive table is the Wisdom Woman herself (v 21). She is food and drink; she is the source of nourishment, life and refreshment. To partake of her, to eat her, to be joined with her, intensifies desire for communion with her. In language that anticipates the eucharistic language of Christians, the poem claims that the more one enjoys her, the more one seeks her, and less worthy desires fall away.

In vv 22-23 the language of metaphor takes a concrete turn, giving tangible content to the metaphorical banquet. Specifically, to eat at her table and to partake of communion with her, means to obey her and to labor with her.

> Whoever obeys me will not be put to shame,
> and those who work with my help will not sin.
> All this is the book of the covenant of the Most High God,
> the law which Moses commanded us as an inheritance for the
> congregations of Jacob (24:22-23).

The second verse above explains the first. The obedience of which Sophia speaks (v 22) is obedience to the Law (v 23), and the labor which she enjoins (v 22) is labor in the study of the Law, the book of covenant of the Most High (v 23). One participates in the festive banquet and lives in union with the Wisdom Woman when one obeys the Law of Israel.

Torah

Sirach's identification of the Law or Torah with Sophia is his most radical and original innovation. When he identifies the Wisdom Woman with Torah, he broadens any previous characterizations of her. He incorporates into her persona, the historical and legal traditions of Israel. Consequently, in his theological vision he brings together previously excluded streams of Old Testament thought under Sophia's mantle. It is through this woman and not through Greek humanism or through the divinities of other religions that the meaning of life is unfolded and where communion with God becomes possible. It is in the Torah of Israel.

Law or Torah is a very broad term in the Book of Sirach as well as in Judaism.[5] Primarily, it refers to the Pentateuch, the first five books of the Bible, which tell the story of God's liberation of the people and of divine protection in bringing them to the Promised Land. In the context of this narrative of rescue and redemption, specific laws teach the people how to relate to God in gratitude and how to show love and mercy to each other. Consequently, Torah is both story and law. The story gives the reasons for keeping the laws. Never did Israel understand Torah as the exacting imposition of a legalistic God. As in the Roman Catholic celebration of the Divine Office, the purpose of practicing of Torah is to sanctify the day and the night, and to bring the community into the presence of God in its work, its prayer, and into every corner of its life.

Torah, therefore, is a relational term, conveying from generation to generation the way of interaction between God and

---

[5]Jacob ("Wisdom and Religion," 255-257); von Rad (*Wisdom*, 244-246); and Crenshaw (*Old Testament Wisdom*, 149-155) discuss the significance and the various manifestations of Torah in Sirach.

people. It includes laws, understood as a guide for living, a way of life. It is "a lamp to my feet and a light to my path," sings the psalmist (Ps 119:105), to be meditated on day and night. However, until Sirach's writing, Torah traditions are singularly absent from wisdom thinking.

In answer to the question, "How can I be wise?," Sirach replies, "Live Torah." Torah fills people with Wisdom, he insists, just as the great rivers irrigate the fields of the ancient world (24:25-26). Torah expresses Wisdom, "for her thought is more abundant than the sea, and her counsel deeper than the great abyss (v 29). By urging obedience to Torah, he exhorts his students to obey, worship and commune with God in all their doings, at every moment of their existence. In doing so, he expands and animates the meaning of Wisdom in Israel. Like the fear of Yahweh, obedience to Torah joins one to Sophia and brings one to God.

Relationship with the Wisdom Woman

In the final poem and supporting wall of Sirach's Book (51:13-30), the Wisdom Woman appears again, this time as the object of Sirach's attentions. Written in a biographical style, the poem is a personal testimony to his pursuit of her, his struggles with her and his joy in relationship with her. Though the poem's origins are disputed,[6] it now functions in the Book to summarize Sirach's instructions and to inspire the youth to follow his example. Like the Poem of the Strong Woman which concludes Proverbs (31:10-31), this, too, is an acrostic or an alphabetic poem. The alphabetic ordering of each of the verses implies that the sage's experiences with

[6]Celia Deutsch, "The Sirach 51 Acrostic: Confession and Exhortation," *Zeitschrift für die Alttestamentliche Wissenschaft,* 94 (1982) 400-409.

Sophia order the chaos of his life and, hence, promise the same for his readers.[7]

In the confessional style of the poem, Sirach reflects as an older man on the relationship which obsessed him from his youth.

> While I was still young, before I went on my travels,
> I sought wisdom openly in prayer.
> Before the temple I asked for her
> and I will search for her to the last.
> From blossom to ripening grape my heart delighted in her;
> my foot entered upon the straight path; from my youth I
> followed her steps.

From Sirach's point of view, this relationship subsumed all the other interests of his life and to it he committed all his energies. No matter how arduous the road, he never abandoned his pursuit of this woman. The passionate language of the poetry, "I will search for her to the last," reveals his dedication to winning her.

Nonetheless, he reports that his own unflinching resolve is insufficient to win her. By praying for her in the temple from the beginning, he acknowledges that she is God's alone to give. Even the decision to follow her, the Sage insists, comes from beyond himself. "My heart was stirred to seek her" (v 21). Despite his extensive efforts to gain her companionship, he pauses in the midst of his poem to credit God for the gift of her. "To him who gives wisdom I will give glory" (v 17). But

[7]Anthony R. Ceresko, "The Sage in the Psalms," a paper presented at a meeting of the Old Testament Colloquium, Conception Abbey, Conception, MO, Dec 12, 1986. For other suggestions about the significance of this form, see his article, "The ABC's of Wisdom in Psalm XXXIV," *Vetus Testamentum* 35 (1985) 99-104.

then he resumes his account of the labor required of him. He "grappled" with Wisdom, he could not learn enough of her, he directed his soul to her. At last, through purification he came to a new level of relationship with her (51:18-20).

According to the sage's account, the wooing of Sophia and union with her involves a tension between human dedication and divine gift. Like the classic witnesses to the spiritual life through the ages, he speaks of the paradox that human effort is both everything and nothing in this search. In the end, only grateful praise and thanksgiving for the undeserved gift remain. With the gift of Sophia came enlightenment, eloquence and the will to praise God. "The Lord gave me a tongue as my reward, and I will praise him with it" (v 22).

Sirach's Invitation

Based on his relationship with Wisdom, Sirach now has the authority to invite others to seek her. Like the sages before him, he knows the truth of his teachings from experience. He claims to be the model, the teacher and the speaker of wisdom, able to guide others along the same path. His account of purifying struggles is designed to inspire and to challenge his audience to the same absolute devotion. Therefore, modeling himself after Sophia, he issues his own invitation, not to a banquet but to another form of nourishment, to a life of study and meditation.

> Draw near to me, you who are untaught, and lodge in my school.
> Why do you say you are lacking in these things,
> and why are your souls very thirsty?
> I opened my mouth and said,

Get these things for yourselves without money.
Put your neck under the yoke,
and let your souls receive instruction;
it is to be found close by (51:23-26).

In this poem, he appeals to the deepest needs of the human person. Hunger and thirst are metaphors here for every condition of deprivation, alienation and incompleteness. To quench their thirst and to alleviate their hunger, he invites them "to put their necks under the yoke."

A common image from Sirach's time[8] the yoke to which Sirach invites his students to submit is the study of Torah. Like an animal yoked to the plow, students of Torah bind themselves over to steady labor and discipline to bring forth a harvest. To begin this labor and to satisfy their hunger, they need not travel to distant places or search the learnings of the world. What they seek "is found close by," in the scriptures of Israel which are within reach of everyone.

Meditation

In Sirach's view, the study of Torah is not only learning but meditation. It is a kind of sacrament in which one meets God anew by meditating on the written word.

Sirach deems study and meditation to be so important that, in this poem and elsewhere in the Book, he encourages his students to follow him in the life of the scribe, devoting themselves to the transmission and interpretation of the Torah. He does not disdain other occupations. Indeed, the labors of the smith, the potter, the farmer "keep stable the fabric of the world" (38:34). But for Sirach, the work of the

---

[8]Deutsch, "The Sirach 51 Acrostic," 406, n 33.

scribe is the most exalted of human occupations (39:1-11). Through it, one is "filled with the spirit of understanding," "one pours forth words of wisdom and gives thanks to the Lord in prayer" (39:6).

However, since Torah and Sophia are nearly interchangeable for Sirach, he can urge with equal fervor that his readers meditate on Sophia herself.

> Blessed is the man who meditates on wisdom and who reasons intelligently.
> He who reflects in his mind on her ways will also ponder her secrets.
> He who peers through her windows will also listen at her doors;
> he who encamps near her house will also fasten his tent peg to her walls (14:20-24).

In this passage, the language of love replaces the language of labor in the description of meditation. To meditate on Sophia is to reflect on her ways with the ardor and the dedication of a lover seeking the beloved. Consequently, meditation is not purely a mental activity, as modern dualisms might suppose, but a life lived in intimate connection with Wisdom. The one who meditates receives nourishment and life in loving union with Sophia who comes to meet her disciple like a bride (15:2). This is another way of understanding what Sirach means by submitting to the yoke.

How shall I be wise? Study Torah; meditate on Torah; commit your life to receive Sophia's instruction. This will bring you Wisdom and this will unite you with the God of mercy. Thus Sirach can complete the third wall of his Book with a blessing for his readers:

> May your soul rejoice in his mercy,
> and may you not be put to shame when you praise him.
> Do your work before the appointed time,
> and in God's time he will give you your reward (51:29).

The Wisdom Woman extends her life to every part of Sirach's house. As the central figure of the Book, she answers the longings of Hellenism and she competes with its solutions to the human problem. In the three major poems about her, Sirach folds his principal themes into her portrait in images flowing in and out of one another so that she appears as many things at once. She is the fear of Yahweh and she is Torah; she is response to God and she is God. In Sirach's portrayal of her she remains beautiful, alluring and elusive, exercising her influence universally and eternally. She is the way of life for all people. However, to meet her one must embrace the traditions of Israel.

Sirach illustrates this point very clearly in cc 44-50 in a long paean which he begins "In praise of famous men and our fathers in their generations" (44:1). (He mentions neither famous women nor our mothers "in their generations.") Listing well-known and lesser known figures of Israel's scriptures, Sirach provides examples of people who lived according to his theological vision. Abraham kept the Law of the most High (44:20). Moses received the commandments "face to face" (45:5). Phineas was "zealous in the fear of the Lord" (45:23). Simon was High Priest, leading glorious worship in the Temple of the Most High (c 50). Each of these great ancestors received blessing and glory; each lived in wisdom and in praise of the God of Israel. So, too, should Sirach's reader.

Practical Advice

Inside the well-constructed walls of his house, Sirach offers practical advice to apply his theoretical vision to daily living. "How shall I be wise?" "How shall I fear Yahweh?" "How shall I live Torah?" His answer is simple, traditional and difficult: "Live in right relationships with others." The bulk of his practical instructions centers on human relationships. Like the sages before him, he speaks as an expert on the subject, but unlike previous wisdom writers, Sirach incorporates his views on human relations into his larger theological vision.

Human Relationships

For Sirach, to recognize and to nourish one's bonds with other human beings is both to practice Torah and to live in fear of Yahweh. Moreover, to deal justly, wisely and lovingly with other people is to live in union with the Wisdom Woman. All three themes, Wisdom, fear of Yahweh, and Torah, have always been relational terms in Israel, but Sirach makes their expression in human relations explicit. In his view, life is a whole fabric, a tapestry in which one can become wise only by fostering life within the human community.

Sirach borrows much of his teachings on human relations from Proverbs. However, he draws together the isolated sayings of Proverbs to shape longer essays on familiar topics, thereby elaborating on and applying proverbial teachings. This procedure accentuates the importance of human relations for him, and it sharpens an inherited spirituality that focuses on the connections among people. This, he insists, is the praxis or activity of wisdom. It is the way to become wise and the expression of wisdom already achieved. Wisdom's praxis grows from a respect for other people that is expressed in mundane instructions on etiquette and in more sublime teachings on solidarity with the afflicted, on regard for the self and on friendship. One's respect for the dignity of others, he advises, should extend to even the most ordinary courtesies.

> The foot of a fool rushes into a house,
> but a man of experience stands respectfully before it.
> A boor peers into the house from the door,
> but a cultivated man remains outside.
> It is ill-mannered for a man to listen at a door,
> and a discreet man is grieved by the disgrace. (21:22-24).

Of course, Sirach's advice on matters of courtesy is not entirely altruistic. Here, and in his amusing advice regarding table manners (31:12-32:2), he recognizes the advantages refined courtesies contribute to his students' success and advancement. However, he is not teaching crass opportunism. His advice about manners is an application of his vision of human connectedness. One treats others with the utmost regard because one is intrinsically related to them. Regardless of their social station, humans are fundamentally connected because they share the same mortal condition. "How can one who is dust and ashes be proud? for even in life his bowels decay" (10:9).

Solidarity with the Afflicted

Because of his appreciation of the bonds among people, and because of social conditions under Hellenism, Sirach is vehement about responsibility to the poor, the disregarded and the afflicted in society. The Hellenist culture of his time neglected social responsibility, substituting economic gain as a high personal value. As it always does, this skewed set of beliefs aggravated the plight of the lower strata of society.[9] To remind his students who come from the comfortable classes of their social responsibilities, Sirach draws upon the resources of the Jewish traditions. In his opinion, Wisdom cannot be gained without fulfilling these responsibilities.

Thus Sirach advises: "Help a poor man for the commandment's sake, and because of his need do not send him away empty" (29:10). In this exhortation, two factors motivate action for the poor. The first is the needs of the poor. To those needs everyone is obliged to respond because all people are related. The second is the law of God. This reference to the Torah motivates believers to recognize that their God requires such action. To help the poor is to live accoridng to Torah, and to practice Torah is to live in the presence of God.

More than charity is expected of the believer.

> Incline your ear to the poor, and answer him peaceably and gently.
> Deliver him who is wronged from the hand of the wrongdoer;
> and do not be fainthearted in judging a case.
> Be like a father to orphans,
> and instead of a husband to their mother;
> you will then be like a son of the Most High,
> and he will love you like a mother (4:8-10).

Active engagement in relieving the suffering of others, delivering the wronged, parenting the orphan, being attentive to the needs of the poor—these activities will make one a child of God whose love surpasses even that of a mother. According to

[9]Hengel, *Judaism and Hellenism*, 56.

this passage, at least, it is these activities that God values more than any other.

In the tradition of the Torah and of the prophets, Sirach's work eliminates all remarks, such as appear in Proverbs, that demean the poor, or blame them for their circumstances. In his writing there is only compassion and respect for them. With uncompromising insistence he teaches that those with resources have obligations to the resourceless.

> Deprive not the poor of his living, and do not keep needy eyes waiting.
> Do not grieve the one who is hungry nor anger a man in want.
> Do not add to the troubles of an angry mind, nor delay your gift to a beggar.
> Do not reject an afflicted suppliant, nor turn your face away from the poor.
> Do not avert your eye from the needy, nor give a man occasions to curse you;
> for if in bitterness of soul he calls down a curse upon you,
> his Creator will hear his prayer (4:1-6).

Needy eyes waiting, fed eyes averted, bitter sufferings and failed community. This is the reality of the world but it should not be, Sirach insists. His picture of the lot of the poor and of the negligence of the comfortable is timeless, repeated around us and by us. Do not deprive the poor of their living; do not turn your face away from the poor, he commands. The systemic problems of our times, Sirach does not and could not address, but on one thing he is clear: the needs of the poor and afflicted are everyone's needs.

In a similar vein, Sirach also departs from proverbial wisdom in his attitude toward wealth. He still holds that wealth can be a relative good, but wealth is not the great good of Proverbs. "Be content with little or much" (29:23), he urges. "The essentials for life are water and bread and clothing and a house to cover one's nakedness" (29:21). That should be enough. In Sirach wealth no longer signifies one's virtue nor signifies divine blessing upon its possessors. Indeed, it may convey the opposite. In Sirach's experience the greed of the wealthy is one of the causes of poverty. He warns, "A rich man will exploit you if you can be of use to him, but if you are in need he will forsake you" (13:4). Moreover, the rich will drain your resources, deceive you and finally deride you (13:5-7).

Regard for Oneself

Sirach does not exclude regard for the self from the network of relationships toward which one is responsible and whose dignity one is to respect. He admonishes, "Do not give yourself over to sorrow and do not afflict yourself deliberately (30:21); "Delight your soul and comfort your heart" (30:23); and "Establish the counsel of your own heart for no one is more faithful to you than it is" (37:13). Though this attitude seems self-evident, and though it is explicitly taught by Jesus in the Gospels, regard for, indeed, love for oneself is too often viewed with suspicion and guilt among religious people. However, for Sirach true self-love is the basis for loving others and for praising God. It is required to be wise.

Friendship

On the subject of friendship Sirach is fluent and eloquent. In this common human experience Sirach discovers profound theological meaning. For him, friendship is not a distraction from God but a gift of God and a symbol of divine-human communion.

> A faithful friend is a sturdy treasure,
> he that has found one has found a treasure.
> There is nothing so precious as a faithful friend,
> and no scales can measure his excellence.
> A faithful friend is an elixir of life;
> and those who fear the Lord will find him.
> Whoever fears the Lord directs his friendship aright,
> for as he is so is his neighbor (6:14-17).

Sirach's exuberance in praise of friendship seems to arise from personal acquaintance with the subject. To call the relations among friends a "sturdy treasure," "an elixir of life," is to identify the extraordinary blessing that enduring bonds with another can be. True friendship where people connect with and empower one another in loyalty and love is like feeling the breath of God. In his estimate, it is truly precious beyond measure. In the process of knowing the other and revealing oneself, one touches the power and the energy of God.

Consequently, Sirach's praise of friendship only makes explicit what is hidden in the love among friends. In his opinion, the quality of friendship expresses the quality of one's friendship with God. Those who fear Yahweh live in friendship with Yahweh, and they receive true friends and are enabled to conduct loving friendship. Perhaps, this is because human friendship, like friendship with God, is the result of deep honesty about oneself, of exposing oneself to the gaze of the other, and thus to be healed and to be set free. This literally enables one to be a healing and freeing friend to another in return, for as one is so is one's neighbor (6:17).

But Sirach is a realist; caution and moderation infuse all of his practical advice. New friends should not be welcomed too quickly. Discernment, even wariness should direct their selection. They must be tested first because not all will prove reliable or suitable for your companion. A friend might give a public show of loyalty when things are going well with you, but betray you in adversity. Moreover, shallow friends all too easily turn into enemies (6:7-12). So he advises, "A new friend is like wine; when it has aged you will drink it with pleasure" (9:10).

Sirach's vision of human solidarity, radical and inclusive as it is, possesses some serious blind spots. From human community he excludes both women and slaves. In this regard, he is a product of his time. Slavery was unquestioningly accepted even in Israel, and women were regarded as property of their fathers, brothers or husbands. Though he does urge care within the accepted social arrangements of his day (33:30; 7:19), he remains the premier misogynist among biblical writers. (For example, see 25:24; 26). The caution that he enjoins so often and so insistently in other matters must be applied to his own instructions on these subjects.

To his question, "How shall I be wise?," Sirach answers, "As much as possible, live in communion with all people." Human relations is the chief arena wherein one pursues Wisdom in daily living. Required first is the recognition of one's bonds with other human beings, and second, actions of respect and love. This is the praxis of Wisdom, the activity without which one cannot gain her, nor live with her. This is the way to Wisdom open to every human being. It is, for Sirach, equivalent to fearing God, obeying Torah and worshipping the God of Creation. Without praxis in the human community, one fails in wisdom and one fails in humanity. His themes, like the flames of a fire, converge in the person of Sophia. She draws then all in under her mantle in a burst of heat and light.

In the end, what Sirach desires for his readers is what the Hellenists desire—that they reach full humanity and achieve all that is given in the human vocation. According to his wisdom, this can happen only in communion with God. Sirach wants only that they live in praise and worship, for this is Wisdom, this is the fulfillment and the highest freedom of humankind. The myriad instructions of his guidebook on how to be wise can be summarized this way:

> Let us fall into the hands of the Lord . . .
> for as his majesty
> so also is his mercy (2:18).

7

THE WISDOM OF SOLOMON
AND THE FULLNESS OF LIFE

The Book of the Wisdom of Solomon was written in the latter half of the first century, B. C., by a learned but unknown wise man, usually called the Sage or Pseudo-Solomon. He wrote in Greek for the Jewish community living in the Hellenist city of Alexandria in Egypt. Like the Book of Sirach, the Book of Wisdom is omitted from the Hebrew canon but accepted in the Greek canon. It too is labeled deutero-canonical by the Roman Catholic and Greek Orthodox communities. The Book divides into three parts: cc 1-5, the Book of Eschatology; 6-9, the Book of Wisdom; and 10-19, the Book of History.[1] To become acquainted with this last of the wisdom books, read cc 1-10 and c 18.

When I began to study the wisdom literature, it was the Book of the Wisdom of Solomon I found least appealing. Cooly abstract and historically distant, its complex Greek writing style and philosophical borrowings removed it from the earthy practicality of Israelite wisdom. However, an event in my life provided me with a door into the Book of Wisdom.

[1]James M. Reese (*The Book of Wisdom/Song of Songs*, Old Testament Message 20, Wilmington: Michael Glazier, 1983) divides the Book into four major units, different from mine not only in number but also in identifying interlocking components among the units.

During the month I planned to write this chapter, my mother died. We had known her death was coming for almost a year. Rapidly approaching and then withdrawing, tantalizing us with hope and dread, death came finally as a relief, an elation of communion, and a heart-smashing grief. Suddenly the Wisdom of Solomon impinged upon me in a most personal way.

The Book of Wisdom is about life, abundant, overflowing, and deeply human, and it is about transcending death. The Sage asks, "What is Wisdom?" and he replies that Wisdom is life, not mere physical existence, but pulsing, vibrant relationship with God that is life unending. At the heart of that life lives Sophia. She enables, blesses and confers life. She is life. This chapter discusses the Wisdom of Solomon from the perspective of life lived in righteousness, life lived forever, and life lived with Sophia. Before turning to these themes, however, it may be helpful to discuss the experience of the community that gave birth to the Sage's complex teachings.

The Ferment in Hellenism

In the late first century B. C., the Hellenist city of Alexandria was a place of religious and philosophical ferment. While the classical Greek philosophies of Plato and Aristotle were disintegrating, religious speculation of every variety sprang up to fill the void. The Sage's Hellenist contemporaries were searching for human perfection, for wisdom, and for the all-embracing powers and deities of the universe.[2]

---

[2]James M. Reese's classic study (*Hellenistic Influence on the Book of Wisdom and Its Consequences*, Analecta Biblica 41; Rome: Biblical Institute Press, 1970) provides a splendid discussion of the pervasive influence of Hellenistic thought and literary forms upon the Wisdom of Solomon.

Advertising slogans of today capture some of the ethos of that ancient world. Among the Hellenists there was an unbridled yearning to live without restraints, "To be all that you can be," "To know no boundaries," to escape somehow the mortality inherent in the human condition so as to live in the world of the spirit. Hellenist proposals to achieve this state were legion. They ranged from Stoicism, to Epicureanism, to the worship of Isis, the great mother goddess of Egyptian wisdom.

This turbulent religious climate threatened the Jewish faith anew. On the one hand, to some of its adherents, Judaism appeared narrowly particular in its faith and practice, as well as suspicious of the world and of whatever is human. For them Judaism failed to compete with the universal appeal of Hellenism. To the Hellenists, on the other hand, Judaism was an unwelcome and barbarian religion, given to exotic rituals and to the worship of a nationalistic deity.[3] Consequently, Jews were treated as pariahs in the sophisticated Alexandrian society. They were mocked, persecuted and ostracized. This maltreatment weakened Jewish confidence in the power of their own traditions even further.

Moreover, the Jews of Alexandria possessed memories lingering from the previous century of Seleucid Hellenists brutally oppressing their ancestors in Jerusalem. To the Sage's contemporaries, therefore, their ancient faith was suspect not only because it could not compete with Hellenism, but also because its God seemed unable or, worse, unwilling to save them from persecution and death. The Sage wrote his Book to

---

[3]David Winston, *The Wisdom of Solomon*, Anchor Bible 43 (Garden City: Doubleday, 1979) 3-4.

reclaim Judaism for the disillusioned and the disedified. He sought to reaffirm the justice of Israel's God and to show that Judaism offered life that surpassed all the promises of Hellenism.

Greek Borrowings

To show that Judaism could compete with, and even transcend, Hellenism's claims, the Sage adopts not only Hellenism's questions but also some of its answers. More than Sirach, the author of Wisdom dips deeply into the language, thought and literary conventions of the Greek circles of his day. His willingness to appropriate Hellenist thinking caused one scholar to declare the Sage a "progressive" theologian in contrast to Sirach's more traditional approach.[4] Indeed, the Sage's work represents imaginative religious thinking at its best. Unafraid of alien or "pagan" culture, he sees in Hellenism kindred strivings, insights and intimations of divine presence in the world. Through this creative process, today called "inculturation," the Sage adapts Israel's faith to the new circumstances of his time and place. His adaptations enable Judaism to survive in its new context, and, in the exchange, to acquire new insights into its own truth.

"Rulers of the Earth"

One of the Greek conventions that the Sage employs is the use of royal titles to address his readers. Calling them rulers, judges and kings (1:1; 6:1, 9, 21), he flatters and inspires

---

[4]Alexander di Lella, "Conservative and Progressive Theology: Sirach and Wisdom," ed. James L. Crenshaw (New York: KTAV, 1976) 401-426.

them.[5] The ruler represented the ideal human being that everyone wanted to be. Perhaps deriving from Plato's idealization, centuries earlier, of "the philosopher king" as the embodiment of human virtue, education and perfection, the monarch became the symbol in Greek culture of every human possibility. By addressing his audience as rulers, Pseudo-Solomon honors them; he acknowledges their yearnings for human perfection, and he exhorts them to embody the virtues of the ideal ruler.

However, more is involved in the Sage's use of royalty than mere Greek convention. His titles serve as a vehicle of his theology. In a prayer in c 9 he speaks of God's purposes in the creation of humanity,

> To have dominion over the creatures thou hast made,
> and rule the world in holiness and righteousness,
> and pronounce judgment in uprightness of soul (9:2b-3).

In the Sage's view, to rule the world is the true vocation of humanity. Hence, to address his readers as rulers and judges emphasizes the dignity and the royalty of all believers. It invites them to accept responsibility for themselves and for their world and calls them to live in right and just relationships.

To emphasize this point, the Sage adopts the role of a ruler himself (cc 6-9), not of the Greek philosopher king, but of King Solomon, the ideal monarch of Israel's Wisdom traditions. By assuming the role of the great patron of Israelite wisdom, he weds the royal aspirations of the Hellenist era to the Jewish scriptures. They, not Greek thinking, provide inspiration for his readers and the true basis for human perfection.

[5]Reese, (*Hellenistic Influence,* 149-150) argues convincingly for a figurative interpretation of these titles, but Winston (*The Wisdom of Solomon,* 100-101) claims that the Sage addresses true rulers.

The Life of Righteousness

For the Sage, the highest royal virtue to which his readers can aspire is the virtue of righteousness. Often translated "justice," righteousness is an ancient and value-laden biblical term.[6] To live in righteousness means to live in just relationships. However, biblical justice involves more than equity. It also means to live in harmony with God during all one's life so that every action and relationship is characterized by loyalty and truth. So important is this virtue to the Sage's agenda that he devotes the first five chapters of his Book to an exhortation to live in righteousness and to avoid its opposite, unrighteousness.

Curiously, the Sage describes justice more by portraying the behavior of the unjust than by delineating justice directly. This is a device that enables him to make a second, more subtle point. Injustice is not some sinful abstraction into which his people might be tempted but an interpretation of the behavior of their present persecutors. His attention to the unjust enables him to explain the causes of the persecution of his people and to give them hope in the midst of it.

Two Kinds of People

According to the Sage's description of them, the just and the unjust form mirror images of one another. Opposites in their thinking, their relationships and their loyalties, one group is entirely good and the other entirely evil; one is devoted to life and the other committed to death.

Initially, this sharp dichotomy between the two categories of people, though arrestingly dramatic, seems to create a false

---

[6]See Reese's discussion of the terms in *The Book of Wisdom*, 26-31.

and even dangerous view of humankind. But the Sage is not making universal claims. He is interpreting a specific historical situation of a persecuted people. To do so, he speaks about the righteous and the unrighteous in the categories of apocalyptic literature.

Apocalyptic Influences

Apocalyptic literature and thinking flourished among persecuted Jews and Christians for four centuries, from the second century B. C., to the second century A. D.[7] Apocalyptic thinking is the product of oppressed peoples. Basic to it is the belief that the evil of a particular historical situation is so overwhelming that only God can rescue the victims and set things right. In truly brutal and hopeless conditions, the oppressed experience evil as a demonic force before which human activity is utterly powerless. In such circumstances, the victims perceive their persecutors as agents of evil powers and, in comparison, they see themselves as innocent prey.

Though the Wisdom of Solomon is not apocalyptic literature, its author borrows from apocalyptic thinking to draw his portraits of the just and the unjust and to promise hope to his persecuted community.

Sound Thinking

The dichotomy between the righteous and the unrighteous appears immediately in the Book's opening poem (1:1-11).

---

[7]For a summary of apocalyptic thinking see Bernhard W. Anderson, *Understanding the Old Testament*, fourth edition (Englewood Cliffs: Prentice Hall, 1986) 619-633; and Gerhard von Rad, *Old Testament Theology*, vol II (New York: Harper & Row, 1986) 300-315.

The first difference between the two groups of people lies in their thinking. In the ancient world where the human person was perceived more wholistically than in western culture today, thinking and acting were considered indivisible activities, different poles of the same human reality. Thinking is joined to action as roots are connected to the limbs of a tree. Therefore, for the Sage thinking and acting are inseparable, and, hence, if one thinks righteously, one will live righteously.

> Love righteousness, you rulers of the earth,
> Think of the Lord with uprightness,
> seek him with sincerity of heart;
> because he is found by those who do not put him to the test
> and manifests himself to those who do not distrust him.
> For perverse thoughts separate men from God,
> and when his power is tested, it convicts the foolish;
> because wisdom will not enter a deceitful soul,
> nor dwell in a body enslaved to sin (1:1-4).

In this passage sound thinking consists of thinking of the Lord and of seeking the Lord with sincerity of heart (1:1). Consequently, this means that sound thinking is relational. The just have knowledge of God and so they also call themselves children of God (2:13, 16). They think soundly because they orient their whole lives toward God, and their every deed grows from this root. From this sound thinking follow just actions of gentleness, forbearance (2:19) and opposition to the wicked and their ways (2:12).

Unsound Thinking

In contrast, the unjust reason "unsoundly" (2:1). They orient their thinking toward themselves and toward death; they have a wrong "consciousness." To illustrate the addled nature of their thought, the Sage lets them speak for themselves. Life is short, sorrowful and meaningless, they say, and individual lives are the senseless results of chance. Afterwards "we shall be as though we had never been" (2:2); not even a memory will endure. "Our life will pass away like the traces of a cloud and be scattered like mist that is chased by the rays of the sun" (2:4). For the unrighteous, Death's powerful presence absorbs all sense from life (2:5), the way the sun saps the rain from the clouds.

A Covenant with Death

The cause of the perverted thinking of the unjust is the alliance which lies at its root. It is to the all-consuming power of death that the unrighteous vow their loyalties and give over their lives.

> But ungodly men by their words and deeds summoned death,
> considering him a friend, they pined away,
> and they made a covenant with him,
> because they are fit to belong to his party (1:16).

To magnify its power the Sage personifies death in this passage. For him death signifies not only the end of individual human life but also all the forces of evil at work in his society. With these destructive and demonic powers the unjust make their pact. They long for death, befriend him and derive their energy from him. Death, in turn, poisons their actions, their lives and their relationships.

Aligned with Death, the unjust have no future and, consequently, they have a warped sense of the present. Lacking a future, they find no reason to live justly in the present. Instead, they become persecutors and tormentors of the just.

"Let us oppress the righteous poor, let us not spare the widow nor regard the gray hair of old age. But let our might be our law" (2:11-12a). Their social dealings, expressions of their covenant with Death, are characterized by distrust (1:2), deceit (1:5), blasphemy (1:6) and lawless deeds (1:9). They have no true relationships; they are separated from God; and from them Wisdom flees (1:6).

Punishment of the Unjust

In the Hellenist world this is already a miserable fate. It means that the unrighteous completely fail to achieve the consuming goals of Hellenist society, union with God and the attainment of wisdom. The Sage, however, has only begun his diatribe. With full confidence he arrives at his goal—to announce the inexorable punishment of the unjust.

> For wisdom is a kindly spirit and
> will not free the blasphemer from the guilt of his words;
> because God is witness of his inmost feelings,
> and a true observer of his heart, and a hearer of his tongue.
> Because the Spirit of the Lord has filled the world,
> and that which holds all things together knows what is said;
> therefore no one who utters unrighteous things will escape notice,
> and justice when it punishes, will not pass him by (1:6-8).

To make emphatic the certainty of their fate, the Sage lists an array of divine manifestations that ensure divine action. Each clause shows that God has full knowledge of events in the world and will not free the guilty.

To the disheartened and wavering Jewish community of Alexandria, this passage proclaims that, no matter how it appears, God does not abandon suffering people nor tolerate injustice toward the downtrodden and afflicted. The just will be vindicated because God is just.

The Sage's images of God as wrathful judge and demanding sovereign are, ironically, theological affirmations of divine justice and mercy. They reveal, on the one hand, that God's anger is directed toward the unjust, the oppressors and destroyers of God's people. On the other hand, these images teach that those society excludes, God gathers in; those ruthless people destroy, God lifts up. The God of Israel will not tolerate the obliteration of the suffering people. To be among the righteous means, for the Sage, to participate in this divine compassion and mercy. By their own choice, the unjust exclude themselves from this mercy and love.

A Mysterious Future

For the just, God's compassion and mercy open a mysterious and glorious future (5:15). In the most original of the Sage's teachings, he announces that not even death is an obstacle for them in their relationship with God.

Hebrew Notions of Death

That death does not abort relationship with God would have been a startling notion for the Sage's community. In the Hebrew thinking, death was something to be dreaded, not because it ends physical life, but because it ends all relationships. Death consigns the individual to Sheol, a place of suspended existence, of shadow and of isolation. In that dark world one no longer participates in the banquet of life with family, friends and kinfolk, and, as the Psalm affirms, one no longer joins in the praises of God. "In Sheol who can give you praise?" (Ps 6:5). At death relationship with God dies too.

However, according to ancient belief the dead gain a modicum of immortality through their children. Children bring one vicariously into the future by passing on one's name and one's memory to the next generation. Particularly tragic, therefore, are those who die in youth before children are born to them, or the barren who have no offspring to remember them.

Immortality

Pseudo-Solomon turns this thinking inside out. In his view, no matter the number of their progeny or its lack, death has no grip upon the righteous. The righteous will live forever. Even those people usually considered lifeless and futureless in Jewish society have a future. The barren woman "will have fruit when God examines souls" (3:13); the eunuch will receive "special favor" for his faithfulness (3:14); and the one who dies early "will be at rest" (4:7).

In the Sage's theology God is the author of life, not death. The God of life gave birth to a world designed to generate goodness and blessing for its inhabitants. Therefore, those who are just, who live in harmonious union with God, will receive immortality.

> God did not make death
> and he does not delight in the death of the living.
> For he created all things that they might exist,
> and the generative forces of the world are wholesome,
> and there is no destructive poison in them;
> and the dominion of Hades is not on earth.
> For righteousness is immortal (1:14-15).

"Immortality," *athanatos,* in Greek, means literally, "not death." That which is immortal, which is "not death," is righteousness. The principal relationship of life, relationship with God which the tradition assumed ended in Sheol, will endure forever. Death of relationship, ending of life, is not God's desire for human beings. God created people "for incorruption" and made them in the divine image of eternity (2:21).

Some of the Hellenists believed that immortality is intrinsic to human nature, but this is not what the Sage teaches. Nor does he propose that immortality is something humans earn by their own efforts. Instead, he teaches that immortality is a gratuitous gift of God, given in grace and mercy to the faithful who will abide with God in love (3:9). However, beyond this, the Sage offers no precise definition of immortality. What is clear is that through the gift of immortality God reverses human circumstances, overturns human expectations and explodes the limitations humans place on divine power and justice. No matter how things appear at the moment, God remains faithful to those who are righteous (3:2). The promise of immortality, therefore, contains the promise of the ultimate vindication of the faithful who suffered or died while the wicked lived in comfort.

To a suffering people who doubt the power and fidelity of God the Sage writes that God will never abandon them. "They will live forever and their reward is with the Lord; the Most High takes care of them" (5:15). In light of this promise their sufferings are a small matter, a test or a little discipline, in which "God has found them worthy" (3:5).

> In the time of their visitation they will shine forth,
> and will run like sparks through the stubble.
> They will govern nations and rule over peoples,
> and the Lord will reign over them forever (3:7-8).

These promises reverse the reality in which the author's community currently lives. In an unspecified future time, the powerless will govern nations and rule over peoples. Those without life according to the society's standards, the childless, the fools who seem mad (5:3-4), the persecuted, the martyred and the insignificant, these, if they live with God, will possess an unexpected future. They will achieve what the Hellenists seek—human life glorious and overflowing. For the righteous will "receive a glorious crown and a beautiful diadem from the hand of the Lord, because with his right hand he will cover them, and with his arm he will shield them" (5:16).

Other Old Testament books speak of an afterlife. The Book of Daniel talks of a mysterious awakening of some to everlasting life and of others to everlasting contempt (Dan 12:2). The Second Book of Macabbees speaks about a resurrection of the martyrs (2 Mac 2:13). However, the Book of Wisdom is the first place in the Old Testament that provides a glimpse of eternal life as the destiny of humanity.[8] Though the Wisdom of Solomon anticipates more clearly than other Old Testament literature the New Testament's teaching of the resurrection of the dead, the wisdom teaching and the New Testament teaching are not the same. The Sage speaks of God's gift of eternal life to the soul, not to the body, as Christian writers will insist.

The New Testament teaching on life after death embraces

---

[8]See Reese's discussion *Hellenistic Influence*, 62-71.

the whole person. It asserts that everyone will be raised from the dead, like Jesus, body and soul. This is not to say that people do not really die. Indeed, death occurs, human life comes to an end, wrenching separation is final. Without articulating it completely, however, the Sage anticipates the hope of Christians that God will raise us from the dead. My mother's death has been given new meaning by the promise of the Sage. He affirms that the Living God wants unending life for the individual and for the whole community of believers. In the death of a loved one, in the myriad psychological deaths of ordinary living, and in the vicious martyrdom of whole peoples, there is a future beyond what we can see. Relationships of love and righteousness never end, for God is able to accomplish what we can neither ask nor imagine. The living God is the God of life, faithful, just and merciful. In this lies our hope.

Wisdom

In the Book of the Wisdom of Solomon the matrix of life, life's enabler, its nurturer and its principal expression, is the Wisdom Woman. In herself, she connects together humanity, God, and the universe in a common fabric of vitality. To humankind she offers her own divine life which enhances human life, which aims at the fulfillment of every person and which overflows with the peace and energy of divine presence.

Since she barely appears in the first five chapters of the Book, her importance for the Sage's vision at first is not clear. When he does turn his attention to her in cc 6-9, it seems as if he is changing the subject, but in reality, he is deepening his subject, for in Sophia the themes of righteousness and immortality find their source. "I will tell you what Wisdom is and how she came to be" (6:22), he promises. The Sage's purpose in cc 6-9 is to reveal Wisdom's true identity so that his readers, the rulers of the earth, will find communion with her and have life to the full.

Explicitly assuming the role of Solomon in cc 6-9, the Sage uses the account of Solomon's prayer for wisdom in 1 Kings 3 as the foundation for his testimony about Sophia. Much of cc 6-9 takes the form of a prayer for wisdom. However, he expands this literary base by mixing in ideas and language drawn from Hellenist writings and, especially, from the liturgical praises of Isis, the Egyptian goddess of wisdom.[9] These cultural borrowings notwithstanding, it is the Sage's own lyrical estimate of Sophia that emerges from these chapters.

To praise her the Sage's imagery accumulates like snow in driving winds. He heaps words on top of one another, weaving and swirling them around her. His themes, too, overlap and dance around one another, leading backward and forward in the Book, as he attempts to expose the dynamic life that radiates from Sophia and to express realities that transcend language.

[9]Ibid., 36-50.

Sophia Herself

Twenty one attributes crowd in upon each other in his effusive description of Sophia.

> In her there is a spirit that is
> intelligent, holy,
> unique, manifold, subtle,
> mobile, clear, unpolluted, distinct, invulnerable, loving the good, keen,
> irresistible, beneficent, humane,
> steadfast, sure, free from anxiety,
> all-powerful, overseeing all,
> and penetrating through all spirits that are intelligent and pure and most subtle (7:22-23).

If the sheer number of qualities, the perfect number seven multiplied by three, does not convey her excellence, her attributes themselves do. Her dynamism, her clarity and her transcendence mark her as a divine being.

However, even this listing of her divine attributes does not exhaust her superiority for the Sage. He continues his litany of praises in the language of suggestion and impressionism. "For Wisdom is more mobile than any motion; because of her pureness she pervades and penetrates all things" (7:24). "Though she is but one, she can do all things, and while remaining in herself, she renews all things" (7:27ab). In these verses the Sage claims that her mobility exceeds movement and that her purity infuses all reality. She is self-contained, yet she reaches beyond herself to renew everything. Inexplicably, she transcends the possibilities of the physical world.

Moreover, Sophia's beauty belies description. Not only is she alluring for aesthetic reasons, "more beautiful than the sun" (7:29a), she possesses an awesome moral beauty.

> Compared with the light she is found to be superior,
> for it is succeeded by the night,
> but against wisdom, evil does not prevail (7:29-30).

Stronger than the powers of evil, she is the ruler and designer of the universe who governs it like a queen. "She reaches mightily from one end of the earth to the other, and she orders all things well" (8:1). She is everywhere, all-powerful and overseeing all, and it is she who puts order, stability and beauty into the universe.

Sophia and God

The Sage's language about Sophia stretches near to the breaking point when he speaks about her relationship with God. Using the Greek word, *symbiosis*, he announces that they live, literally, "the same life."

> She glorifies her noble birth by living with (*symbiosis*) God,
> and the Lord of all loves her.
> For she is an initiate in the knowledge of God,
> and an associate in his works (8:3-4).

In similar ways, all four lines of this poem depict the intimacy of Sophia's life with God. She shares "the same life" with him; he loves her. Similarly, she has knowledge of him, that is, according to biblical tradition, she relates to him as intimately as to a spouse. Finally, this mutuality extends even to their divine works as they share a symbiosis of being.

Separate poetic figures, God and Sophia live one life.

> For she is a breath of the power of God,
> and a pure emanation of the glory of the Almighty...
> For she is reflection of eternal light,

> a spotless mirror of the working of God,
> and an image of his goodness (7:25-26).

As close to God as his breath, she is his reflection; she emanates from him; she is his image. She is "God's holy spirit from on high" (9:17). Both Sophia and God are named by the Sage as the one who instructs him in the secrets of the universe (7:17, 22). To see her, therefore, is to see God. To relate to her is to relate to God. She is God, not a new god or a second god, but God poetically imaged as woman. She is Sophia-God.

For the Hellenist society where wisdom was sought in myriad ways, this proclamation of Sophia's identification with the God of Israel proclaims that one can find true wisdom only in the traditions of Israel, only by faith in the God of Israel. In the Book of Wisdom Sophia-God absorbs and appropriates Hellenism's competing claims to wisdom, and she extends her life to all who are willing to meet her.

Friendship with Sophia-God

Sophia-God is accessible, not hidden. Eager to join with her beloved disciples, she energetically pursues them.

> She is easily discerned by those who love her,
> and is found by those who seek her.
> She hastens to make herself known to those who desire her.
> He who rises early to seek her will have no difficulty,
> for he will find her sitting at his gate (6:13-14).

She seeks out friends, waiting for them, appearing to them in their paths, and meeting them in their every thought (6:16). Her initiative in befriending human beings indicates that no one need hold back or feel unworthy of such a friendship. Her gaze of love recognizes the dignity and worthiness of all humanity.

What is necessary for believers to begin this relationship is simply "the most sincere desire for instruction"; this is "the beginning of wisdom" (6:17). This disposition of humble openness sparks a series of actions that brings believers to communion with her. Desire for instruction, says the Sage, is the same as loving her, and love of her is expressed by keeping her laws. Moreover, according to his spiraling logic, to keep her laws or her Torah brings one near to God and assures one of immortality and of a kingdom (6:17-20). These ascending steps summarize the phases of Sophia-God's relationship with her friends.

Pseudo-Solomon's prayerful testimony about his relationship with Sophia elaborates both the requirements and the benefits of this friendship with Sophia. Because he wants to insist upon her identification with the God of Israel, the Sage pays less attention to the role of human choice than earlier wisdom writers, but decisive choice is still important. Besides being open to her instruction, her friends must follow Pseudo-Solomon's example and pray to receive her love.

> I prayed and understanding was given me;
> I called upon God and the spirit of wisdom came to me.
> I preferred her to scepters and thrones,
> and I accounted wealth as nothing in comparison with her
> (7:7-8).

Pseudo-Solomon's prayer reveals the inadequacy of mortal effort in acquiring Wisdom. Beyond human reach, she remains divine gift, self-bestowed gift. Even the most disciplined and schooled practitioners of Hellenistic wisdom fail to gain anything if God does not grant her Wisdom to them.

> For even if one is perfect among the sons of men,
> yet without the wisdom that comes from thee he will be
> regarded as nothing (9:6).

Benefits of Friendship with Sophia-God

Communion with Sophia benefits her friends in every way imaginable. Her friendship is "an unfailing treasure" because "those who get it obtain friendship with God" (7:14). As the friend of humankind Sophia-God empowers and augments human life. Though in cc 1-5 the Sage frequently images God as sovereign lord and angry judge to convey his justice and compassion for the persecuted and martyred, in cc 6-9 the Sage's purpose changes and so does his theological emphasis. In these chapters he is concerned with divulging how Sophia-God richly enhances ordinary existence. She neither dominates nor terrifies her friends, nor does she demand childish or rote obedience from them. Instead, she accords them high dignity, and in befriending them, she encourages them to realize their potential and invites them to join in the richness and excitement of community of life in her beautifully designed universe.

The Gift of Immortality

However, Pseudo-Solomon's images of divine human relationship are even more expansive. Sophia-God marries her friends. Representing every believer, Pseudo-Solomon lives in symbiosis with Sophia (8:9) in the same way she lives with God. Pseudo-Solomon sets up house with her; she is his companion and his life with her (symbiosis) "has no pain, but gladness and joy" (8:16). It is precisely this commingling of lives, this mutuality of love, gladness and joy, which will endure beyond death. "Because of her I shall have immortality, and leave an everlasting remembrance with those who come after me" (8:13).

> For in kinship with Wisdom there is immortality,
> and in friendship with her, pure delight,
> and in the labors of her hands, unfailing wealth,
> and in the experience of her company, understanding,
> and renown in sharing her words (8:17-18).

Material Blessings

Her benefits to her friends include material well-being. Though the Sage values her love more than power, wealth, beauty or health, though he chooses her over the good things of the earth, Sophia, mother of all blessing, gives him these things as well (7:7-11). The material blessings that Sophia-God bestows on her friends are expressions of her love for them. Human needs of food, shelter, health, and human desires for beauty and pleasure are not hindrances to solidarity with her, but gifts from her. These earthy blessings symbolize the plenitude of life that she desires for all peoples. Her gifts are not meant to create a powerful elite who live in comfort while others struggle for life, food and dignity. The Sage decries that way of life in his first five chapters. Rather, implied in his vision is a world of social peace, a society of justice where all are "the rulers of the earth" and where everyone celebrates and shares in the earth's goodness.

Because Sophia-God is the orderer and designer of the universe, she can benefit her friends by revealing its secrets to them.

To know the structure of the world and the activity of the
elements;
and the beginning and end and middle of times,
the alternations of the solstices and the changes of the seasons,
the cycles of the year and the constellations of the stars,
the nature of animals and the tempers of wild beasts,
the powers of spirits and the reasoning of men, the varieties of
plants and
virtues of roots;
I learned both what is secret and what is manifest,
for wisdom, the fashioner of all things, taught me (7:17b-22a).

As much as modern people seek to solve the mysteries of the
universe, so did the ancient Hellenists. The instruction of
Sophia-God reveals the truth their philosophers and religious
groups sought so passionately. To know "what is secret and
what is manifest," how the parts of the world and its inhabitants connect and interrelate, and where humankind fits
within—that was their quest. The Sage answers that the
Wisdom Woman, the "fashioner of all things," alone teaches
this.

Sophia-God as Savior

Again and again the Sage illustrates to his community that
the vital questions of their times are answered in the Jewish
tradition, rearticulated and developed by him in the language
of his contemporaries. Sophia-God is what they are all looking
for. She holds everything together. She embodies all that is
valuable in existence.

But the Sage insists she is not a new discovery of his
generation, nor is she the invention of his creative intellect.
She has been active on the part of humankind since the
creation of the first human beings.

> Wisdom protected the first-formed father of the world,
> when he alone had been created;
> she delivered him from his transgression,
> and gave him strength to rule all things (10:1-2).

From the beginning of human life, Sophia-God empowered human beings to "rule all things," to live in responsible care of the earth and of all its inhabitants.

The Sage devotes most of the remainder of the Book (cc 10-19) to the retelling of biblical history from Adam (he omits Eve and her sisters) to Moses. (An excursus on divine mercy occurs in 11:15-12:22 and an excursus against idolatry in cc 13-15.) The central and saving figure of that history is Sophia-God. In cc 10 and 11 he refers to her as Wisdom and in the remaining chapters as God, but since he has already established their identity as one and the same, his argument is not confused. His purpose is to demonstrate that she has guided, assisted and delivered her chosen people through hardships and horrors from the beginning of history. She will continue to do so.

Throughout these chapters he pays special attention to the events of Exodus. In that prototypical saving event, Israel was oppressed and persecuted by unjust people and systems and then ultimately rescued and vindicated by the mercy and justice of God. In midrashic style, that is, in dramatic elaboration and application of the original story, the Sage relates Israel's history, giving it great immediacy to the current situation of his own community.

> The experience of death touched also the righteous,
> and a plague came upon the multitude in the desert,
> but the wrath did not long continue (18:20).

Like the present community, their ancestors faced death at the hands of the wicked, and, like them, this generation will be saved from the grip of death by Sophia-God. The Sage appeals to the past to assure his readers that the same God who "has not neglected to help them at all times and in all places" (19:22), is still with them, to rescue them from persecution and to lead them into communion of life with her that is everlasting.

EPILOGUE

Wisdom in the New Testament

To study the wisdom literature of the Old Testament is to provide oneself with new eyes with which to read the New Testament. When the early Christians were looking for language and concepts to express their experience and understanding of Jesus after the resurrection, one of the sources to which they turned was the wisdom literature.

Of course, the wisdom literature was not the only resource the Christians used to speak of the Christ event, nor even the primary one. The prophets, the psalms and the historical traditions of Israel provided language and ideas that enabled Christians to begin to speak of their faith in the Christ. However, the Christian communities saw in the wisdom literature, especially in the Books of Sirach and the Wisdom of Solomon, important resources for understanding and describing their new life in Christ. The purpose of this epilogue is to point to some areas of research in the New Testament's use of the wisdom traditions and to suggest possible implications of that research.

Early Christian Hymns

Scholars observe that wisdom language, images and ideas
appear in every layer of the New Testament traditions from
the earliest stages of pre-Gospel writings to the highly developed theology of the Gospel of John. The Christological
hymns of the New Testament are one example of early
wisdom Christology. These are hymnic materials that pre-
dated but are now embedded in the New Testament literature
(Phil 2:6-11; 1 Tim 3:16; Col 1:15; Eph 2:14-16; Heb 1:3; 1
Pet 1:20; 3:18, 22). Used by the Christians in their liturgical
celebrations, these hymns represent the earliest known efforts
of the community to express its faith and to articulate the
meaning of Jesus Christ in their lives. While the wisdom
traditions employed by these hymns are drawn from farther
afield than the Old Testament itself, the hymns utilize wisdom
motifs to express the Christian belief in the cosmic rule of
Jesus Christ. The hymns proclaim that Jesus, like Sophia (Sir
24), preexisted his historical incarnation, lived in intimate
relationship with God (Jn 1:1) and is now exalted and
enthroned in heaven (1 Tim 3:16 and Heb 1:3; 1 Pet 3:22; Col
1:15-20: and Phil 2:6-11).[1]

The Q Document

Another instance of early Christian use of wisdom motifs
before the final writing of the Gospels is in the document
called Q. Scholars believe Q was a collection of the sayings of

---

[1]Elizabeth Schüssler Fiorenza provides detailed discussion in her article,
"Wisdom Mythology and the Christological Hymns of the New Testament" in
Aspects of Wisdom in Judaism and Early Christianity, ed. R. Wilken (Notre Dame:
University of Notre Dame, 1975) 17-51.

Jesus that circulated independently among the communities and was later used by Matthew and Luke in preparing their accounts of events. Though reconstructing the contents of Q is a speculative endeavor, as a collection of sayings Q was probably created as a wisdom genre itself. Q is thought to have depicted Jesus as the final envoy of Sophia, and in its latest stages to have identified Jesus with Sophia.[2]

The Gospel of Matthew

It is particularly in the Gospel of Matthew where the representation of Jesus as Sophia incarnate is developed in a Sophia Christology.[3] For Matthew, Jesus is Wisdom incarnate. Just as Sophia came to earth in the Torah (Sir 24) Matthew implies that she becomes present in the person of Jesus. Just as the Wisdom Woman extends an invitation to her disciples (Sir 24: 19-22; 51:26; Provs 9:1-6), so Matthew depicts Jesus inviting his followers to come to him.

> Come to me all who labor and are heavy laden,
> and I will give you rest.
> Take my yoke upon you, and learn from me;
> for I am gentle and lowly in heart,
> For my yoke is easy and my burden is light (Mt 11:28-30).

Similarly, in Matthew's Gospel Jesus' rejection by his own bears resemblance to Sophia's rejection by the people.

[2]See James M. Robinson, "Jesus as Sophos and Sophia; Wisdom Tradition and the Gospels" in *Aspects of Judaism*, 1-16.

[3]M. Jack Suggs, *Wisdom Christology and Law in Matthew's Gospel* (Cambridge: Harvard University, 1970). Accepting Sugg's view, John P. Meier (*The Vision of Matthew: Christ, Church and Morality in the First Gospel*, New York: Paulist, 1979, p. 78, n. 57), cautions, nonetheless, that wisdom influences in Matthew can be overdrawn.

> O Jerusalem, Jerusalem, killing the prophets and stoning those
> sent to you,
> How often would I have gathered your children together
> as a hen gathers her brood under her wings, and you would not.
> Behold your house is forsaken and desolate (Mt 23:37-39).

In the Sermon on the Mount, Matthew identifies Jesus as the true Torah just as Sophia is Torah incarnate in Sirach 24. Moreover, for Matthew the disciples of Jesus are commissioned as envoys of Wisdom incarnate to continue his work. Finally, Matthew's use of the image of the house throughout the Gospel suggests to Miriam Frances Perlewitz,[4] the house of the Wisdom Woman (Provs 9:1-6), where she sets her table to bring together all people. Like Sophia, Jesus' rule erects a house for all the peoples of the earth, Jews and Gentiles alike.

Jesus as a Wisdom Teacher

Throughout the three synoptic Gospels Jesus is portrayed as a wisdom teacher. His entire style of teaching reflects that of the sages. Before his audience he places parables and wisdom sayings that tease the mind. They invite the hearers into a puzzle that leads to a new level of insight. Like the sages and like the Wisdom Woman, Jesus invites the hearers to decide for him or against him, to seek the reign of God or to elect their own death-dealing folly.

The parable is itself a form of wisdom literature, a *mashal,* an implied comparison, "intended to be obscure." The purpose of a parable is "to instruct or more accurately to move to

---

[4]See her volume on Matthew's Gospel in this series.

decision or action."[5] Jesus' use of parables and his representation as a wisdom teacher are not without significance for his
mission. His method of teaching implied a most respectful
regard for the dignity, intelligence and freedom of his audience.
He teaches to persuade, never to coerce or arrogantly to lord it
over his listeners. In this respect Jesus' pedagogy conveys his
message of inclusive discipleship.

The Centrality of the Wisdom Banquet

It was Elizabeth Schüssler Fiorenza[6] who observed the
predominance of meals and festive banquets in the teaching
and praxis of Jesus. Schüssler Fiorenza argues that this is no
coincidence, not even simply Jesus' appeal to a common
human experience. The sharing of meals is a key revelatory
aspect of Jesus' mission.

It is in Jesus' own festive table sharing, not in the cultic
meal, nor in the abstinence of the Baptist, who came "neither
eating nor drinking," that the reign of God is disclosed.
Proclaimed a glutton and a drunkard, Jesus' participation in
meals with tax collectors and sinners, the outcast and the
marginated, was a principle reason for his rejection by his own
people and a shocking revelation of the ways of God.

Moreover, in the many parables about meals and banquets
Jesus reveals "the inclusive graciousness and goodness" of

[5]Madeleine Boucher, *The Mysterious Parable: A Literary Study*, The Catholic
Biblical Quarterly Monograph Series 6 (Washington, D. C.: The Catholic Biblical
Association of America, 1977) 25.

[6]*In Memory of Her: A Feminist Theological Reconstruction of Christian Origins* (New
York: Crossroad, 1983) 118-120 and 130-140.

God.[7] Schüssler Fiorenza points out that Jesus proclaims the God of all-inclusive love who accepts everyone and grants blessing and well-being to all. These are the characteristics of the Creator God, the Sophia-God of the wisdom traditions. Jesus' announcement of the rule of God in parables and images of the meal further elaborates the inclusive invitation he extends to his followers in the name of Sophia-God.

People of every kind are invited to the festive banquet table of God's rule. They come from the highways and the byways; they are the rejected, the unwashed and the insignificant. At this feast it is unnecessary for anyone to ask for a higher seat. All, from the least to the greatest, have equal honor at the table. Those serving the table are the leaders of the community. They lay no heavy burden on the guests; they do not lord it over them, they are not called by honorific titles. For this royal banquet, this marriage feast, symbolizes the rule of God already present in Jesus and in his mission. The meal sharing of Christians, therefore, is a feast celebrating and actualizing the radical inclusiveness of Sophia-God. For the One who prepared the banquet sent out her disciples to call from the highest places so that all could hear,

> "Whoever is simple turn in here!"
> To him who is without sense she says,
> "Come and eat of my bread and drink of the wine I have mixed"
> (Provs 9:3-5 and see Sir 24:19-22).

The Gospel of John

Finally, one of the latest New Testament writings, the Gospel of John, utilizes the previous articulations of wisdom

---

[7]Ibid., 119.

Christological thinking to produce highly developed incarnational Christology. Building upon the work of Raymond Brown, Elizabeth A. Johnson summarizes John's identification of Jesus with Sophia in this way:

> Like Sophia, Jesus calls out in a loud voice in public places, and speaks in long discourses using the first person pronoun; like Sophia he invites people to come, eat and drink, making use of the symbols of bread and wine; he teaches divine truth and makes people friends of God, particularly instructing disciples and calling them children; like Sophia he is identified with Torah, which is light and life for human beings; those who seek and find him (as with Sophia) are promised the gift of life; he is rejected in ways that spell death for the rejectors.[8]

John's Gospel underscores that the "Word became flesh and dwelt among us" by employing the wisdom traditions of Israel. It was these which helped to prepare the Jewish followers of Jesus to understand the epiphany of God in their world in the historical person of Jesus of Nazareth.

The recognition that the New Testament reapplied Israel's wisdom traditions to help articulate its understanding of Jesus is of more than historical interest. Hermeneutical implications follow. For instance, to recognize the presence of the Old Testament wisdom tradition in the New Testament is to be reminded again of the continuity of faith between the two testaments. It recalls to Christians our Jewish origins and identity, developed, expanded and fulfilled in God's revelation in Jesus. Consequently, for Christians to belittle or demean Jews is to harm ourselves.

[8]"Jesus, the Wisdom of God: A Biblical Basis for Non-Androcentric Christology," *Ephemerides Theologicae Lovanienses,* LXI, 4 (1985) 261-294. This article provides a fine survey of the wisdom tradition into the post-biblical period.

To recognize wisdom influences in the New Testament is to understand in a renewed way the central importance of the banquet table and eucharistic sharing. It invites us anew to work for the full participation of all peoples of the earth in the festive meal of earthly blessing and well-being.

Moreover, the recognition of wisdom imagery in some of the earliest forms of Christology shows that the gender of Jesus does not possess an absolute theological significance. That Jesus was a man is beyond dispute, but to place undue importance on that fact is pointless. Wisdom Christology recalls to us Jesus' radical invitation to be a community of inclusive discipleship, and it reveals the distance we are from that reality.

To notice that Jesus himself taught according to the manner of the sages, winning rather than coercing his listeners, is to be challenged not only by his words but also his reverence and respect for everyone. Perhaps, too, it suggests a pedagogy that might make God's rule more visible in our midst by acknowledging the dignity, responsibility and freedom of each believer. Finally, to recognize that the God whose love and mercy Jesus came to reveal is both Father and Sophia-God, enables us to glimpse less idolatrously, the transcendent and liberating mystery of God.

Biblical Index

BIBLICAL INDEX

Old Testament

New Testament

SUBJECT INDEX